Ginger Mayerson Collage 2012 and 2013

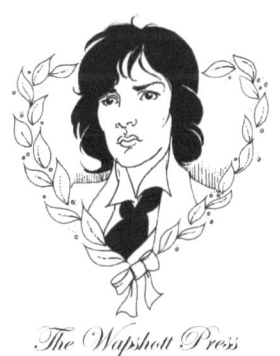

Ginger Mayerson Collage
2012 and 2013

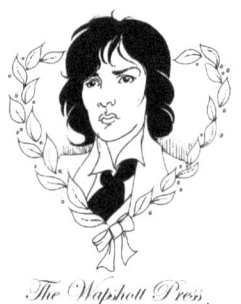

Published by
The Wapshott Press, LLC
PO Box 31513
Los Angeles, CA 90031
www.WapshottPress.com

Copyright © 2012, 2013, and 2016 by Ginger Mayerson

First printing February 2016

All rights reserved. No part of this is publication may be reproduced or transmitted in any form or by any means, electronic or mechanical, including photocopy, recording, or any information storage and retrieval system now known or to be invented, without permission in writing from the publisher, except by a reviewer who wishes to quote brief passages in connection with a review written for inclusion in a magazine, newspaper, or broadcast.

ISBN: 978-1-942007-08-1

06 05 04 03 4 3 2 1

Ginger Mayerson Collage
www.collage.gingermayerson.com

Wapshott Press logo by Molly Kiely

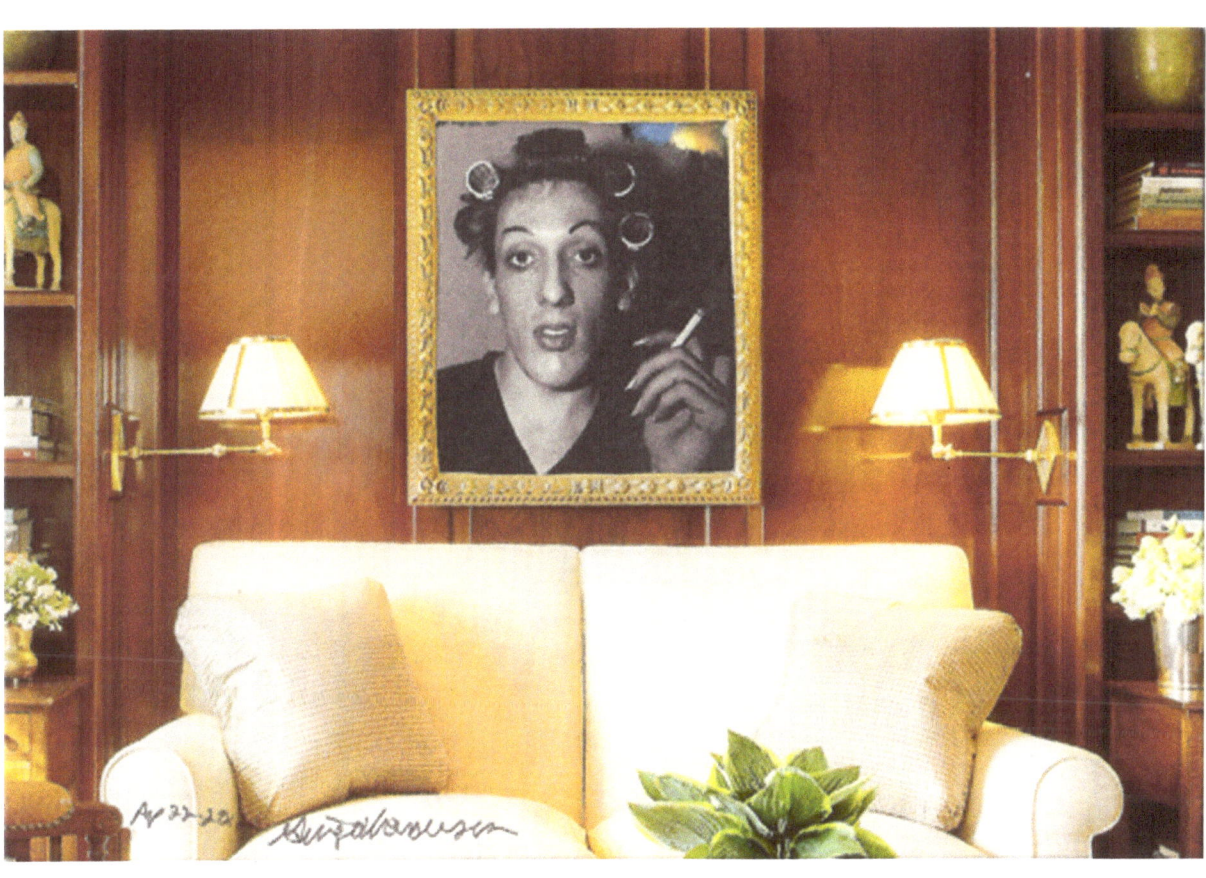

As I was also saying to Diane… 4x6″

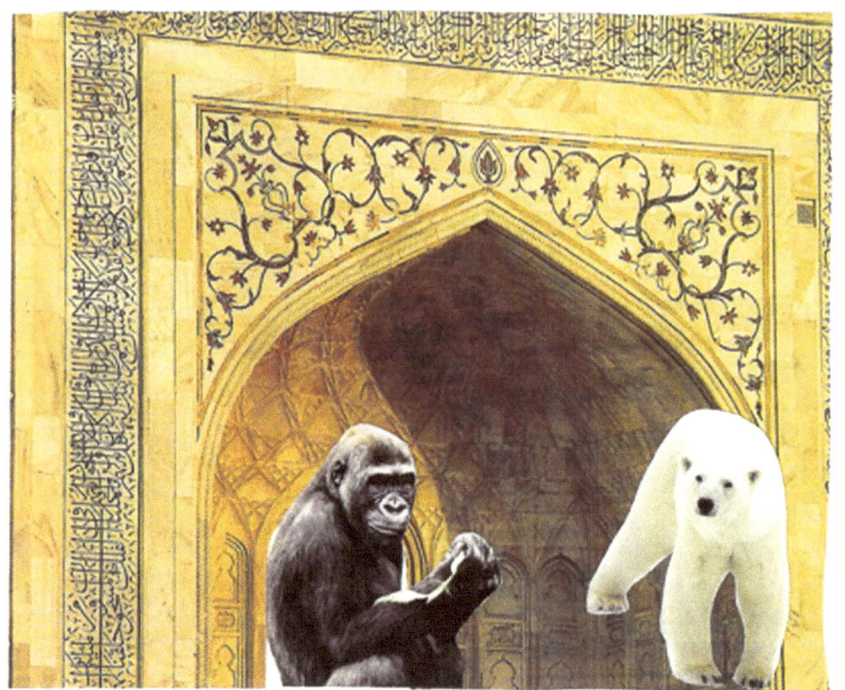
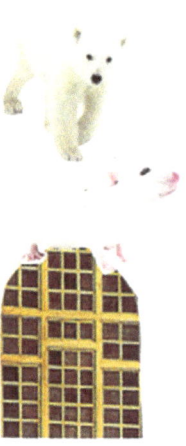

Architecture, 4x6"

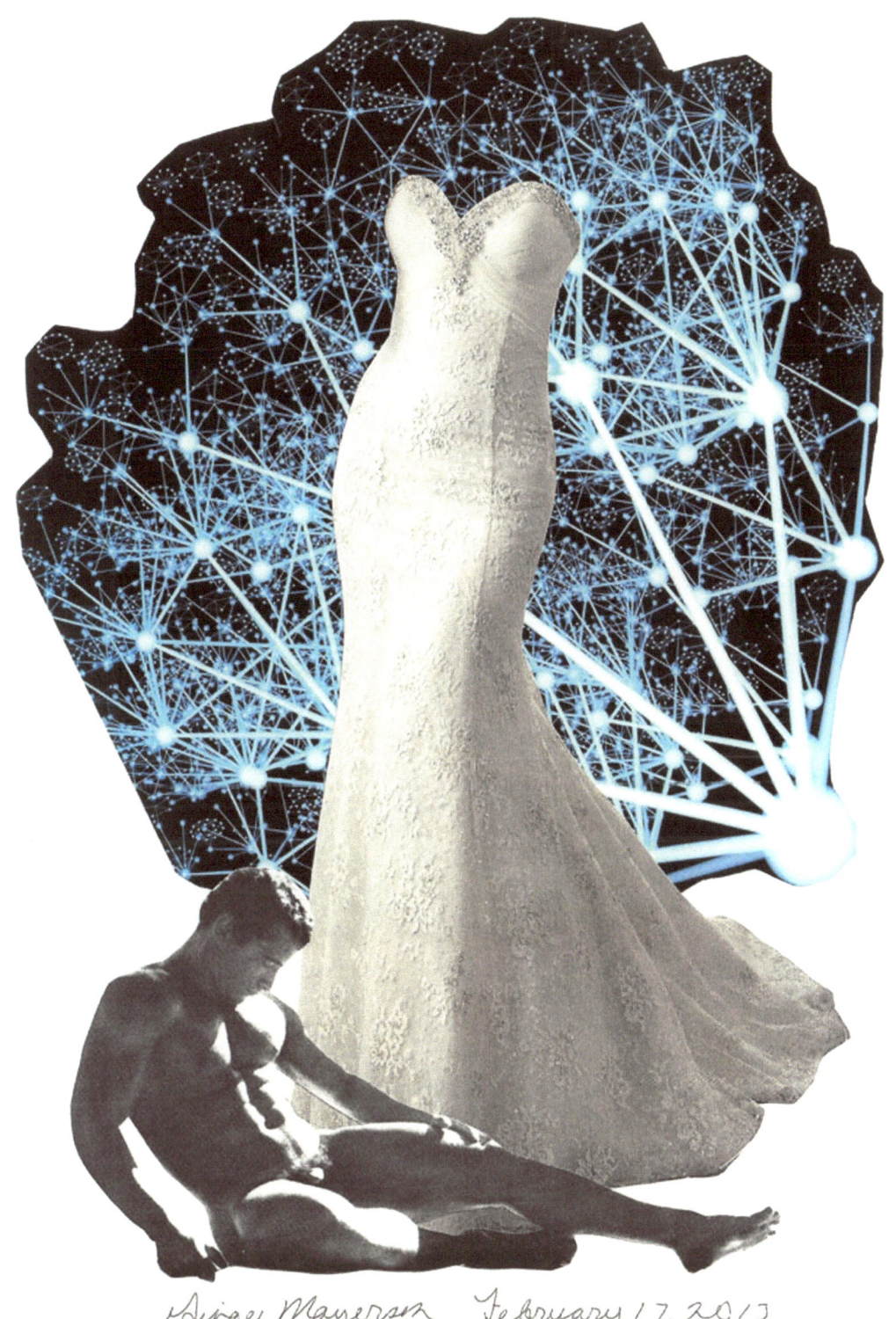

Astro Dress, 10x7"

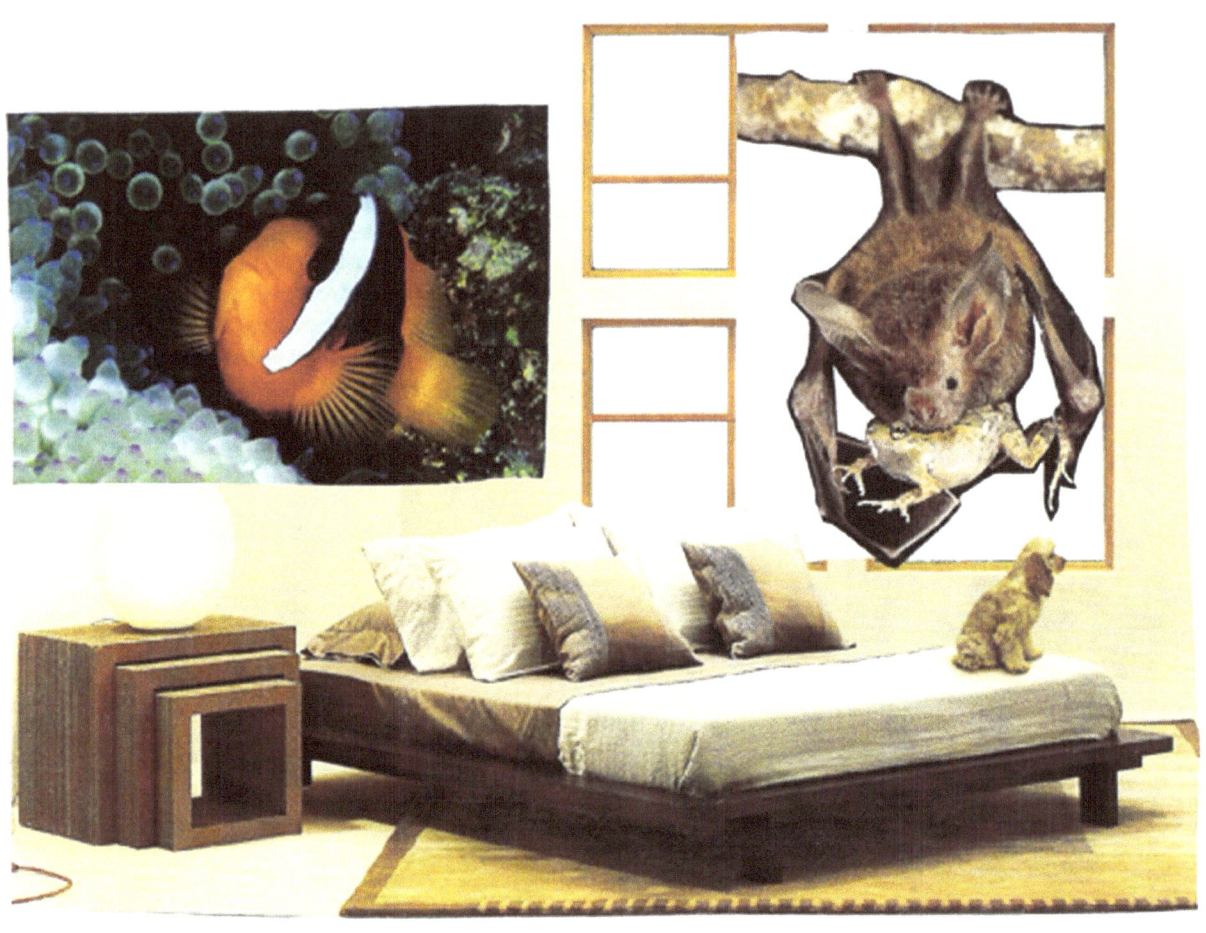

Bats in the Bedroom, 4x6"

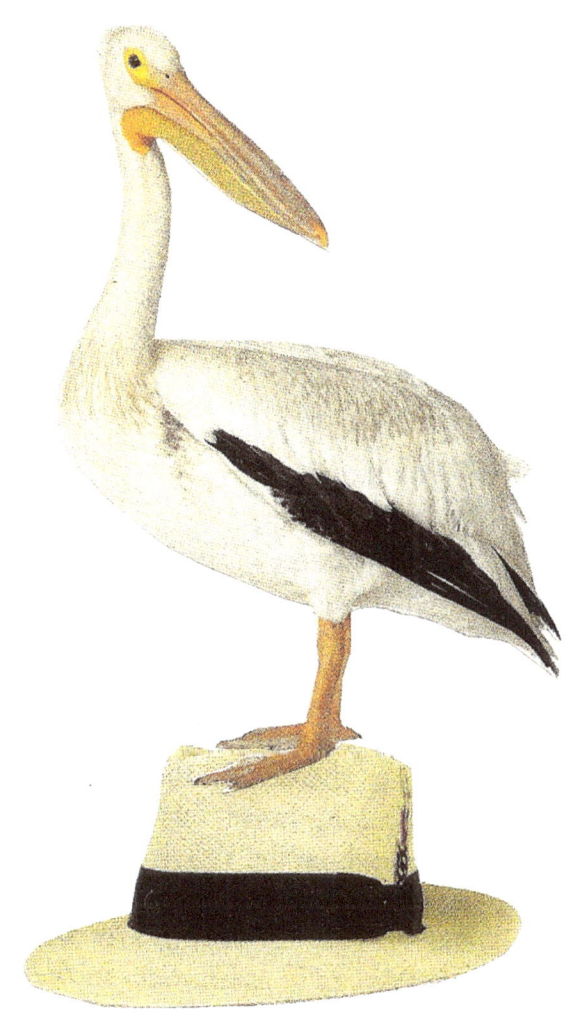

Bird Hat, 6x7"

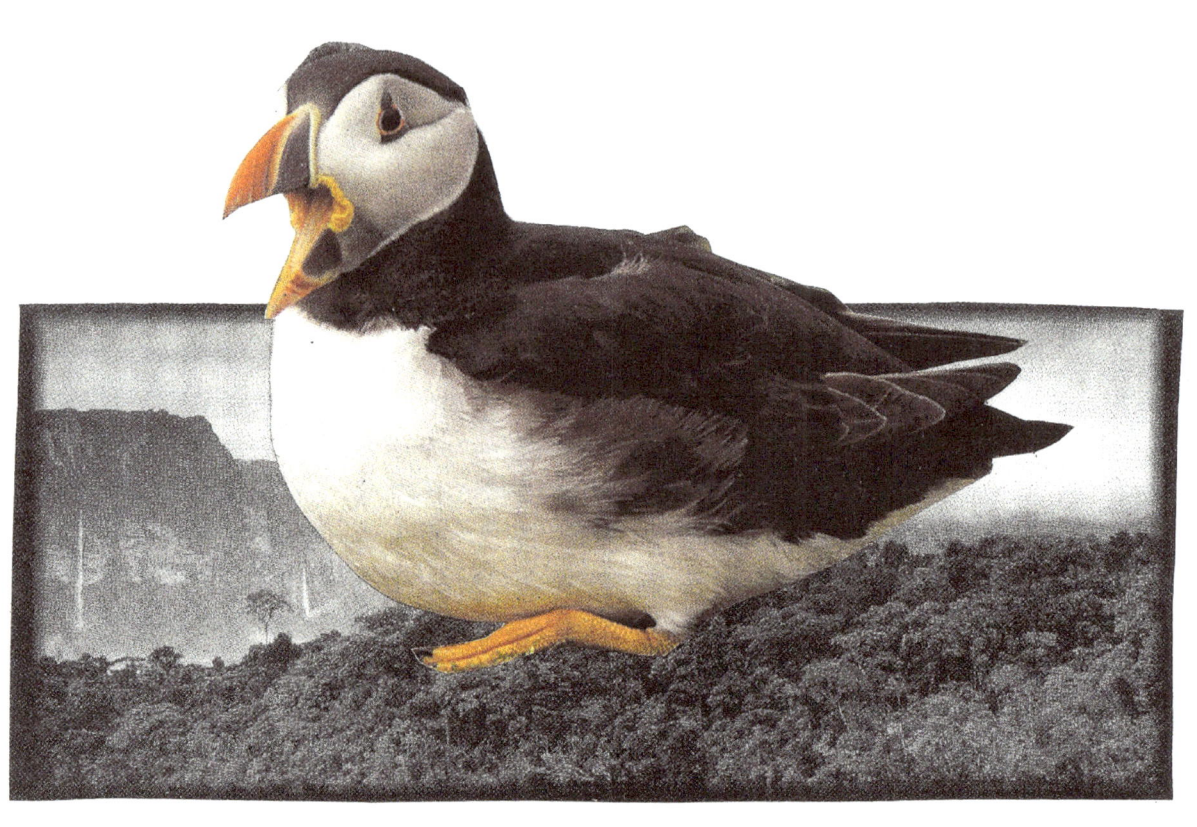

Black and White Bird, 4x6"

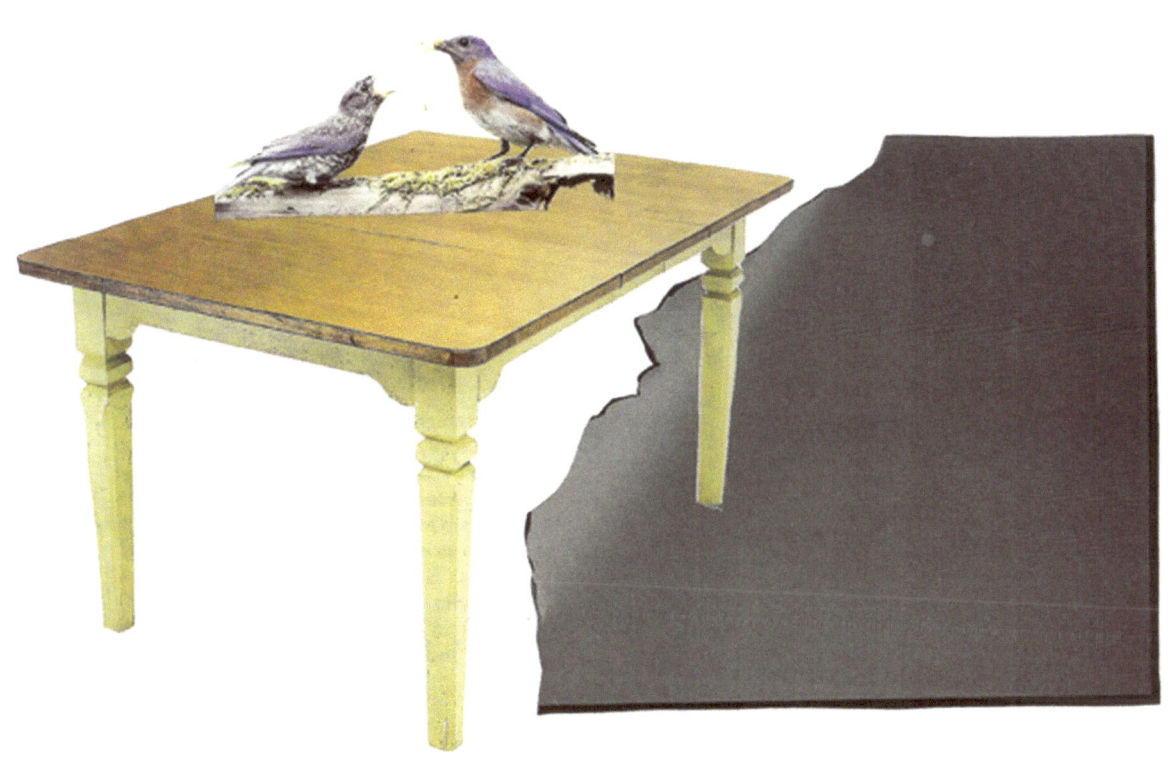

Legend Birds on the Table, 4x6"

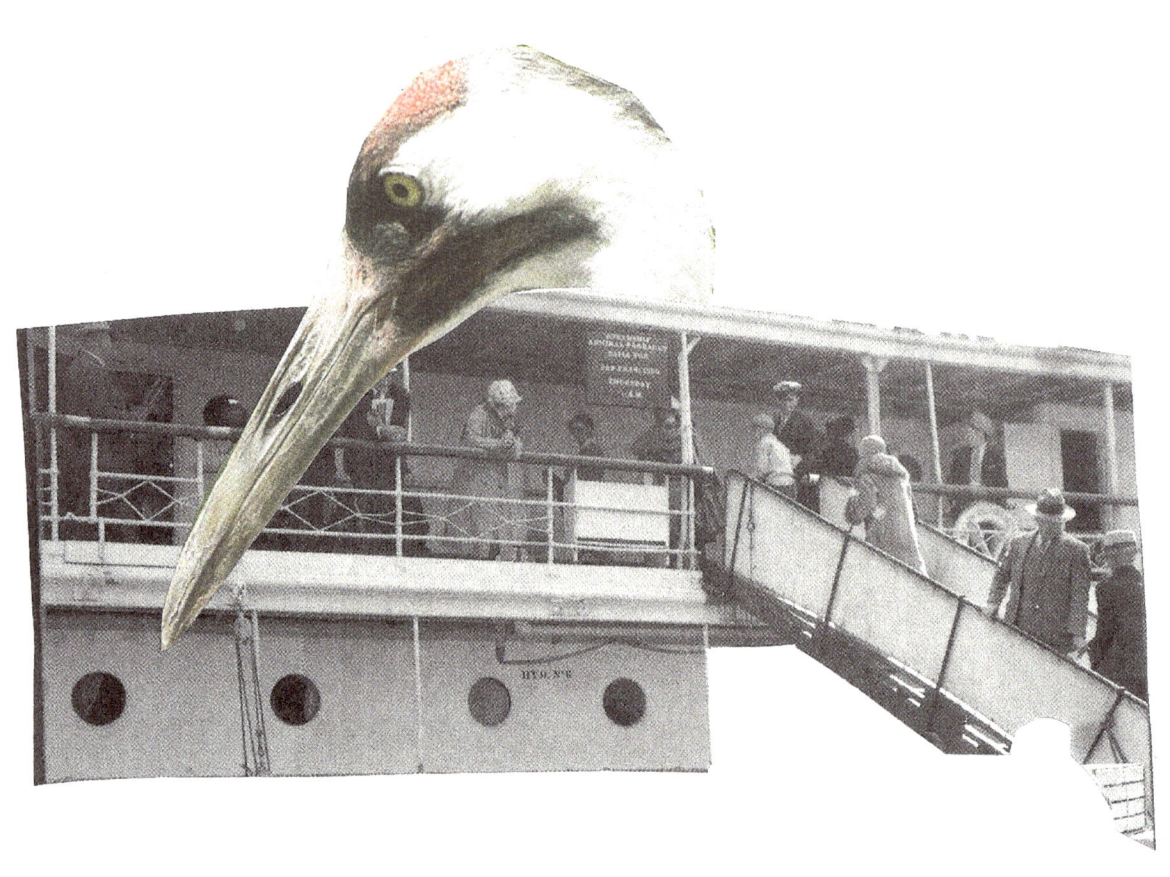

Bon Voyage, 4x6"

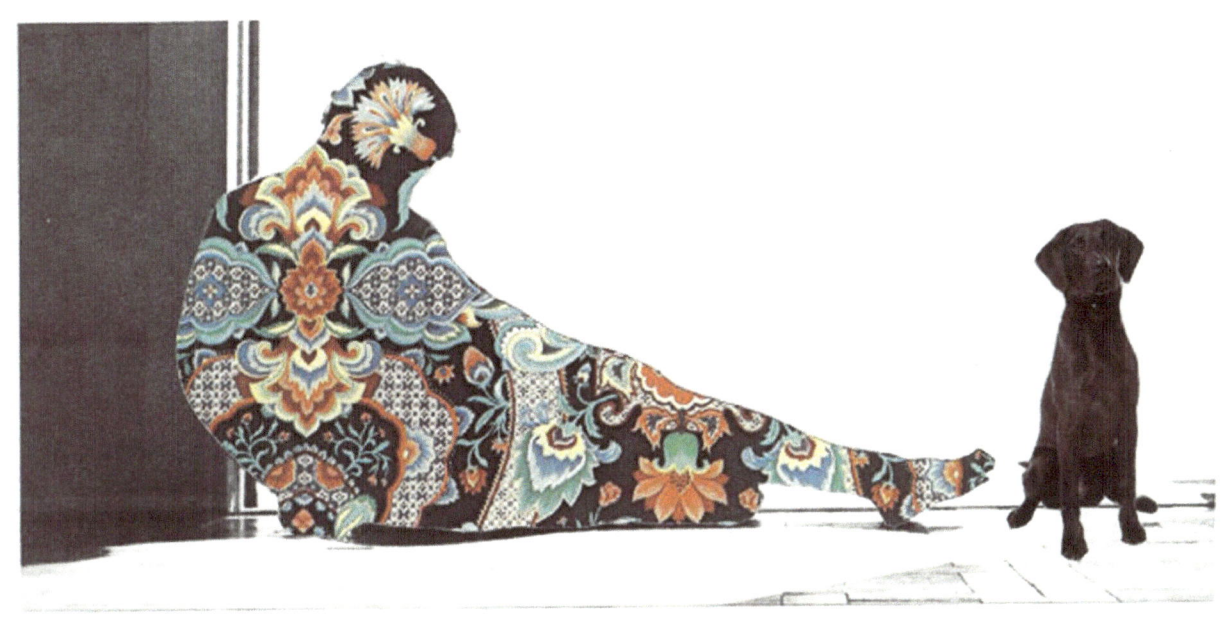

Black Dog's Best Friend, 5.5x8"

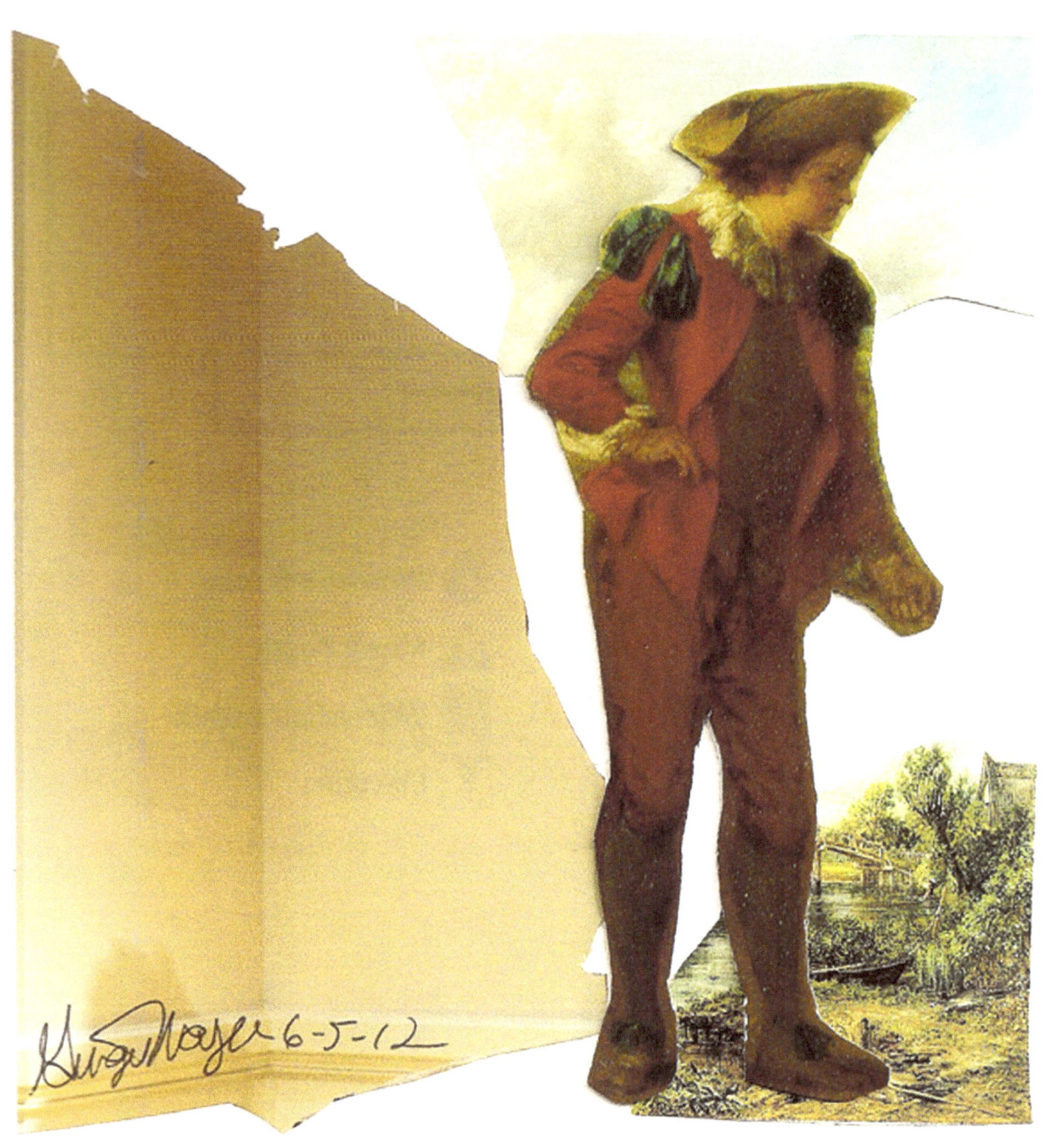

Boy, 5.5x5.5"

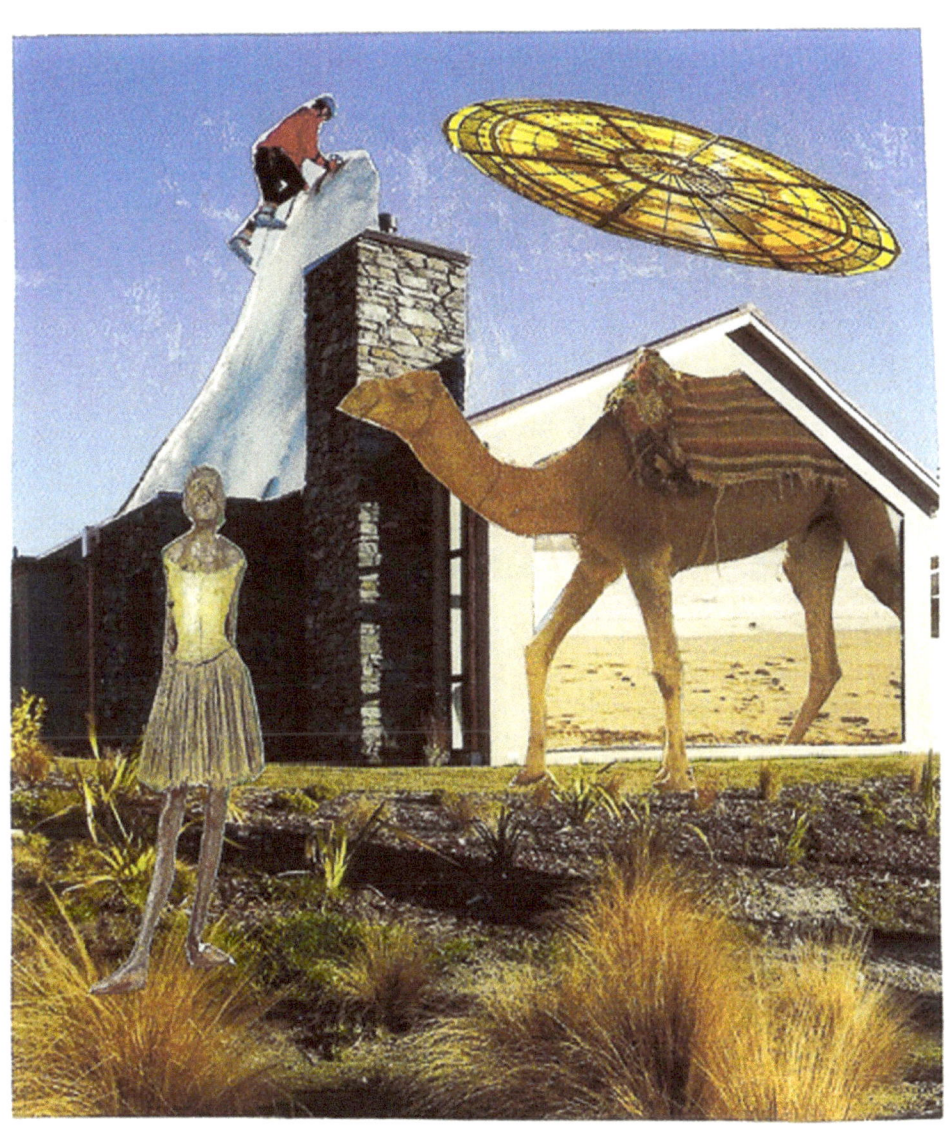

Camel Dancer, 5.5x5.5"

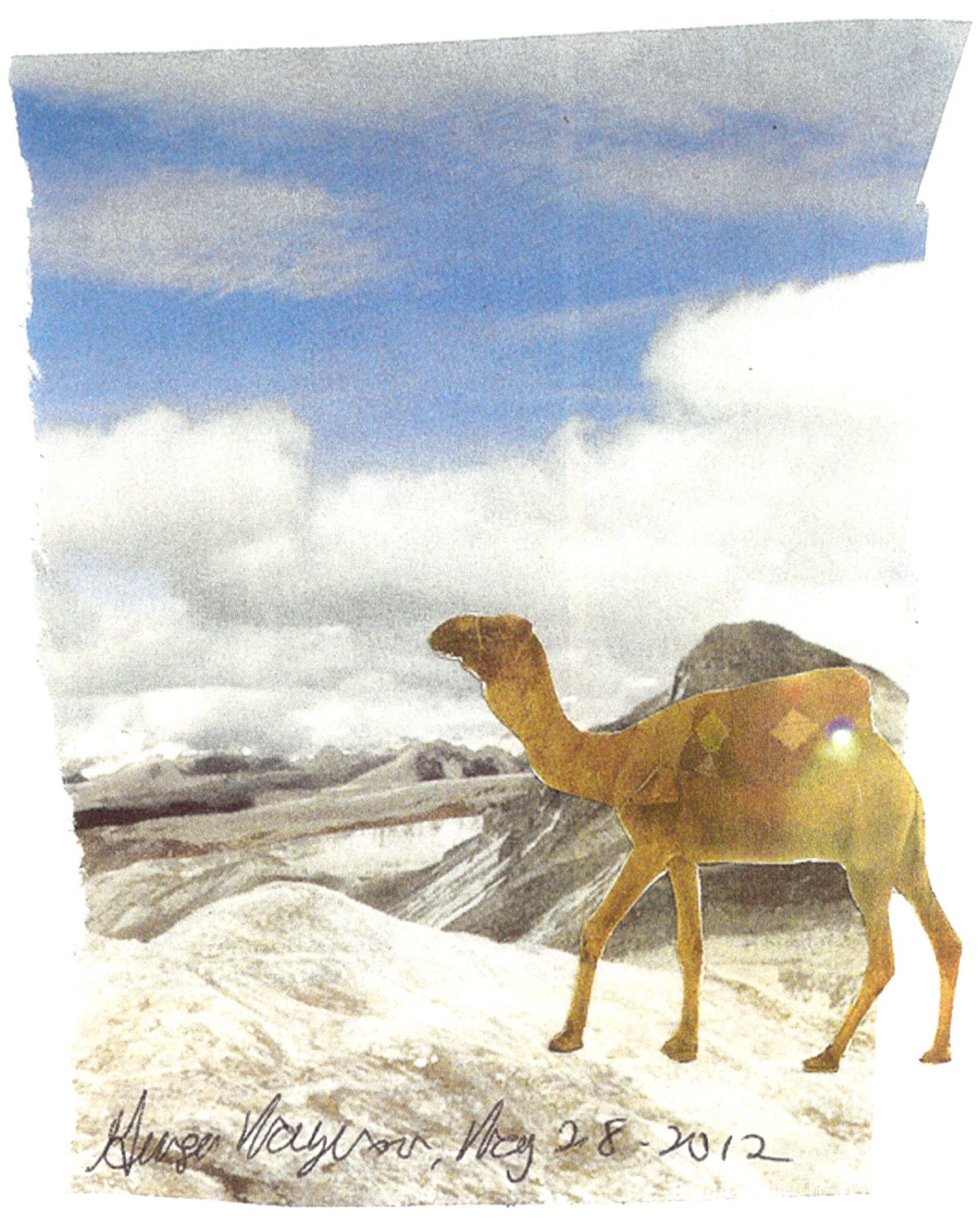

Camel Sky, 5.5x5.5"

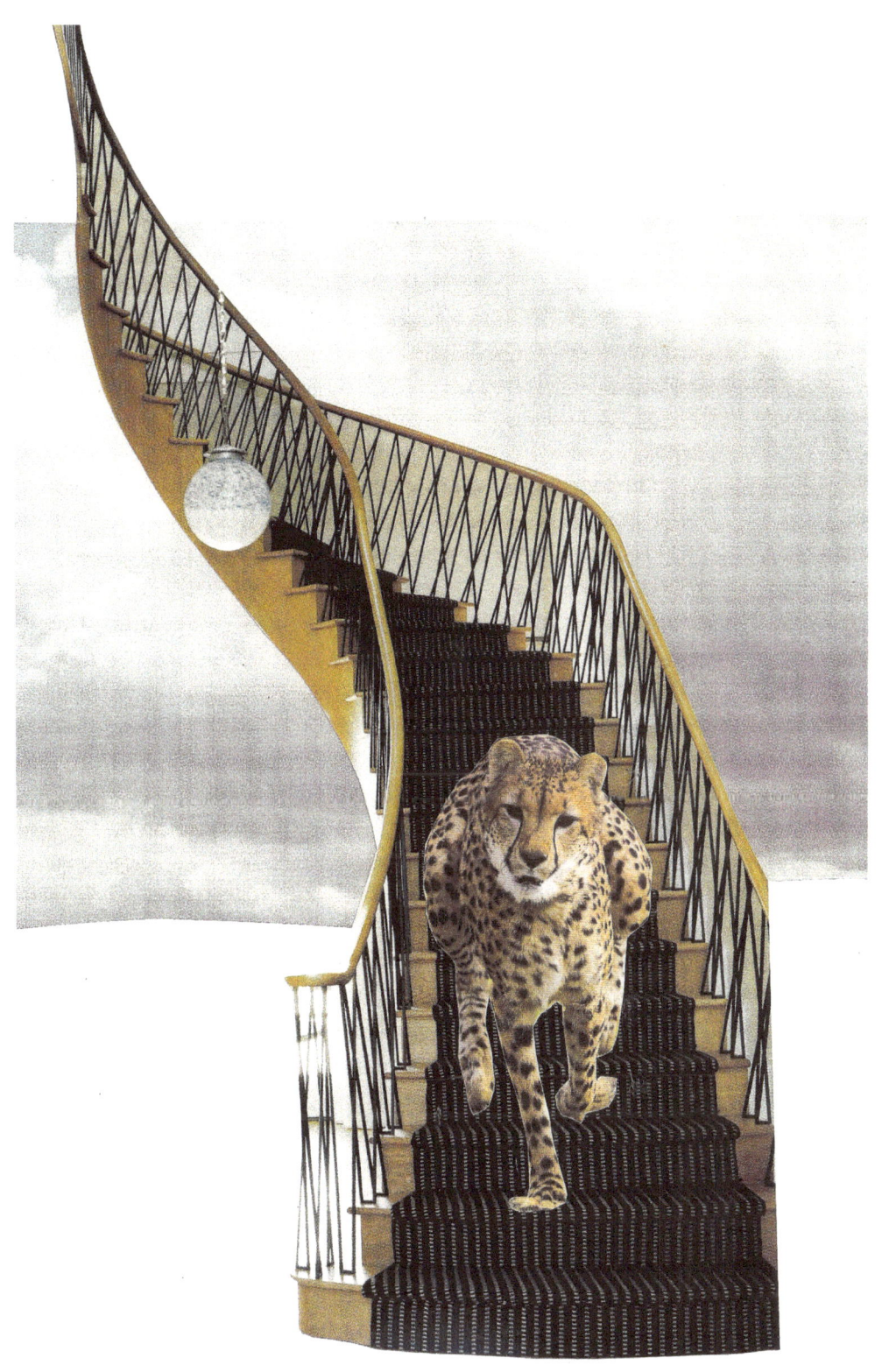

Catcase, 10x7"

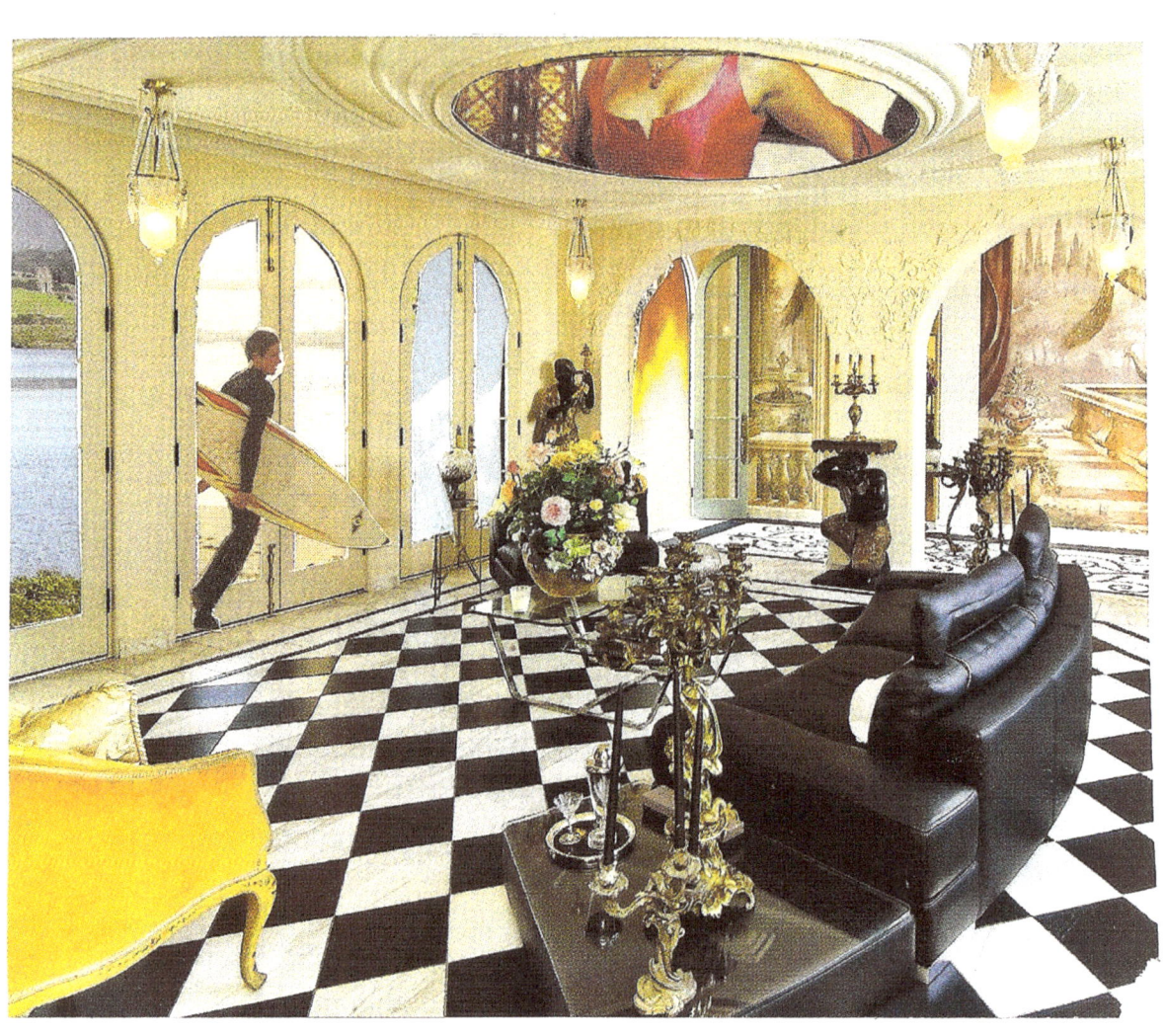

Checkered Floor, 5.5x5.5"

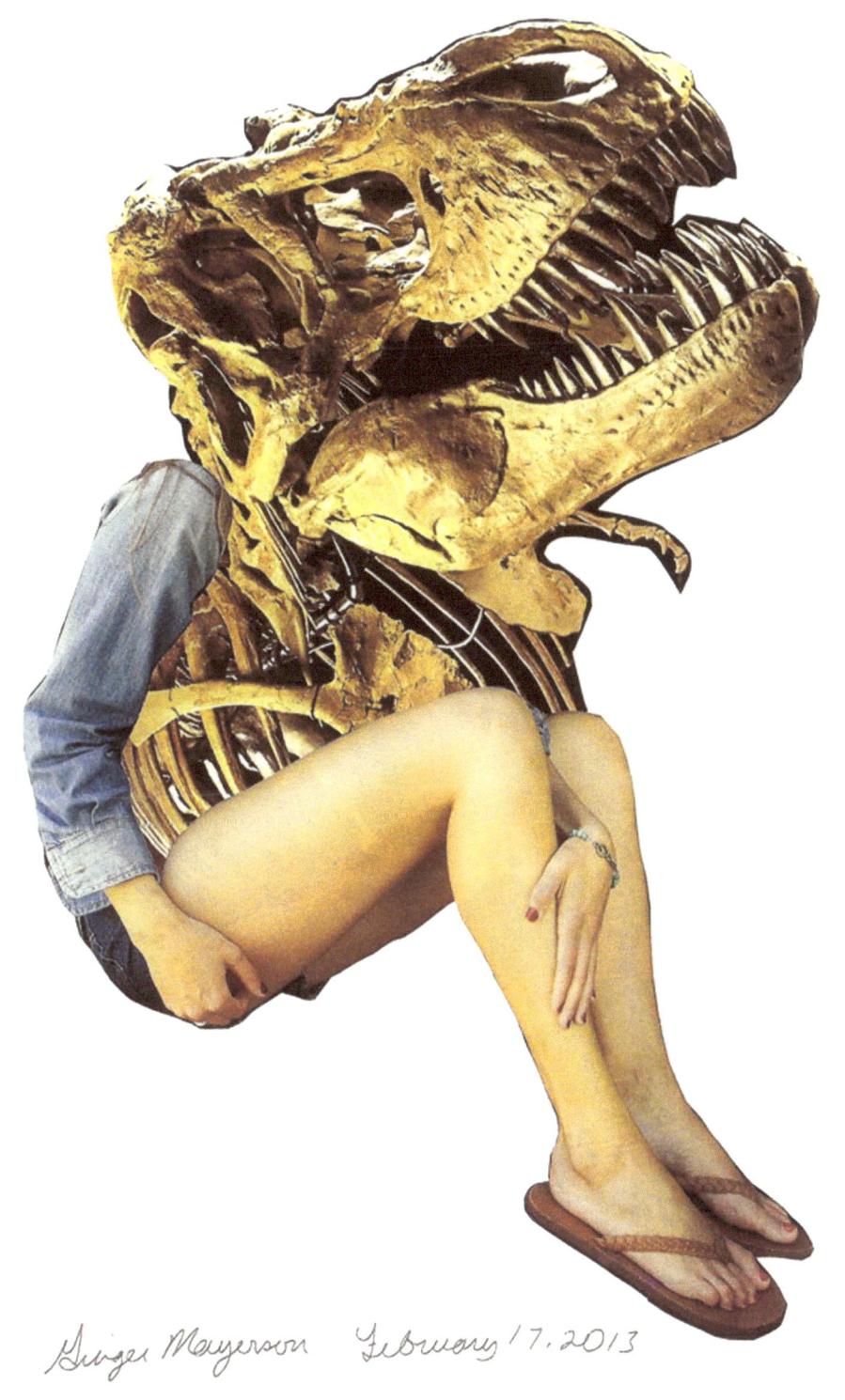

Dino Girl, 10x7"

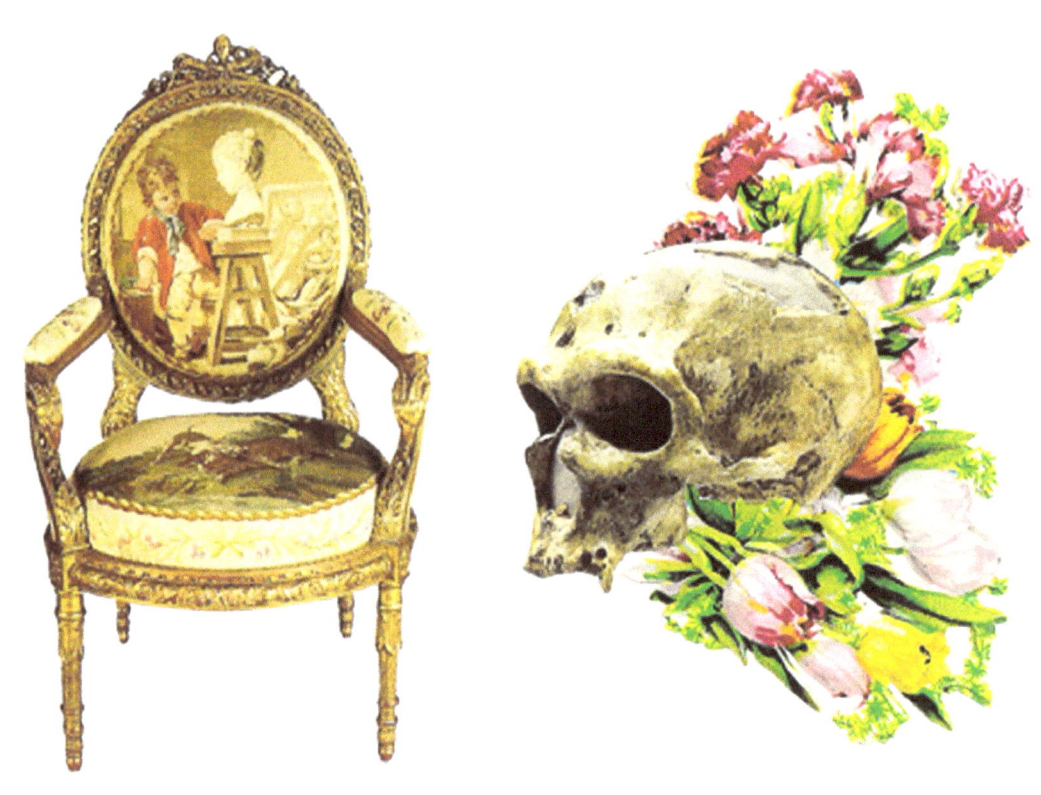

Décor, 4x6"

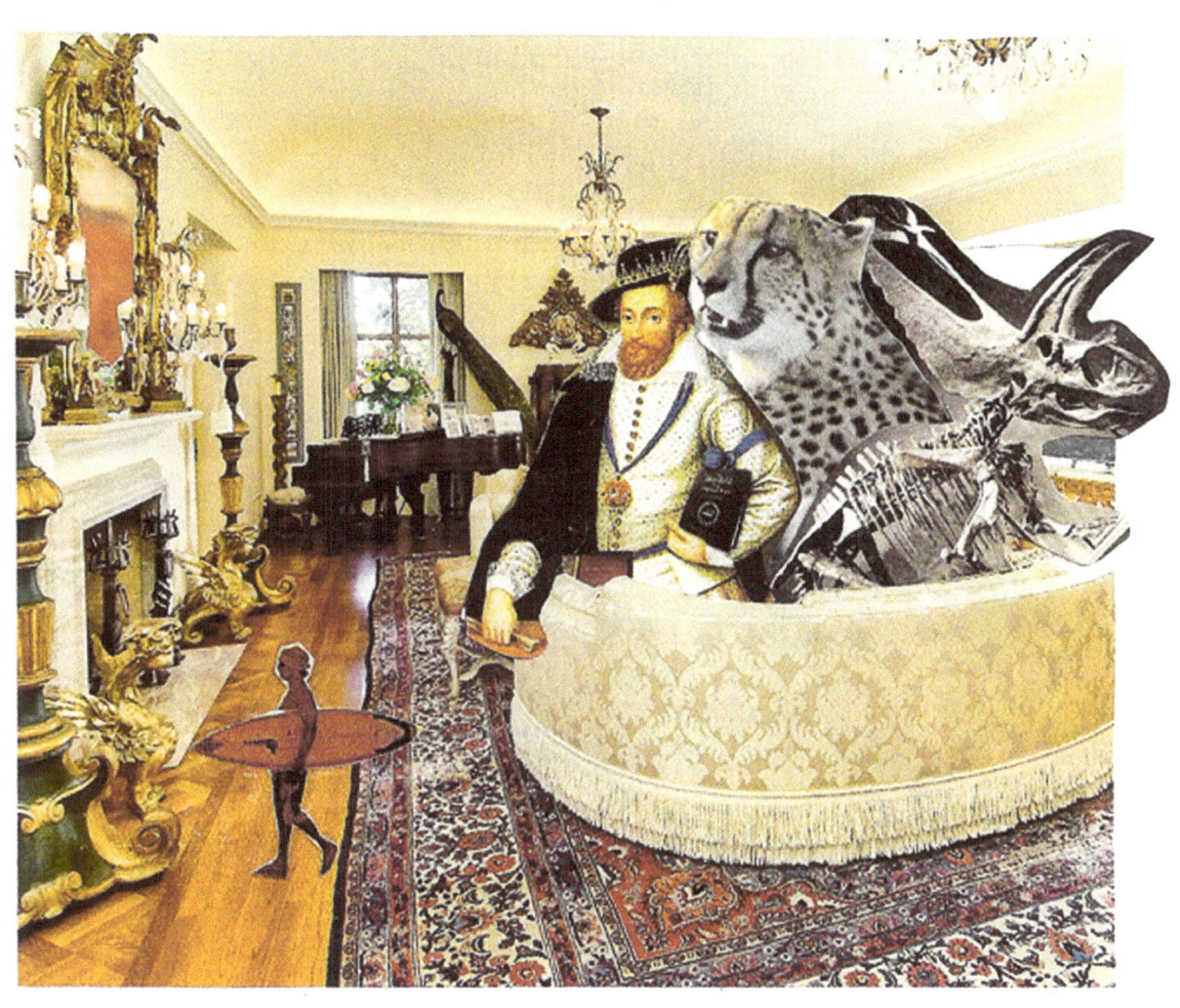

Dino Couch, 5.5x5.5"

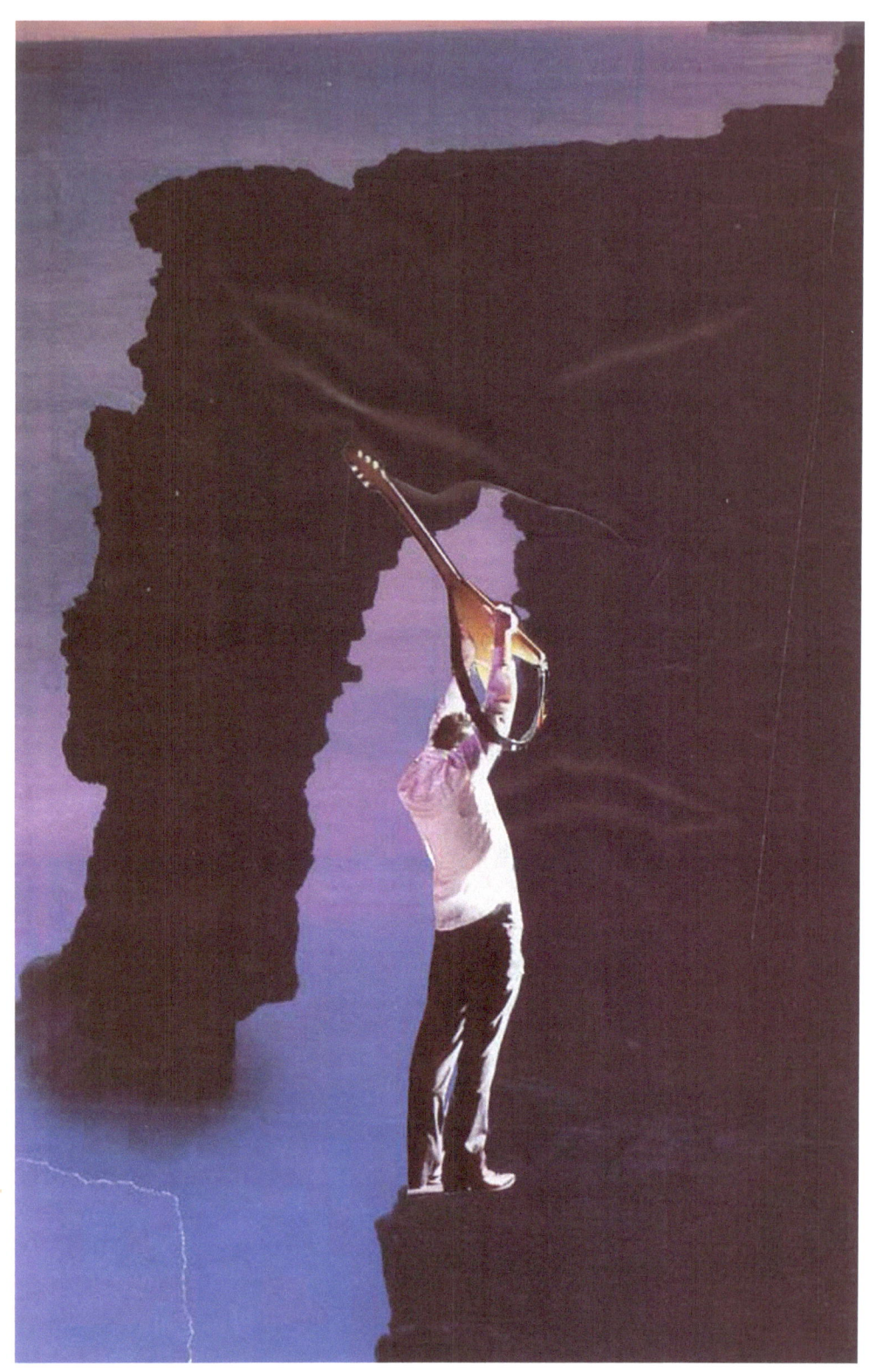

Cliffhanger, 10x7"

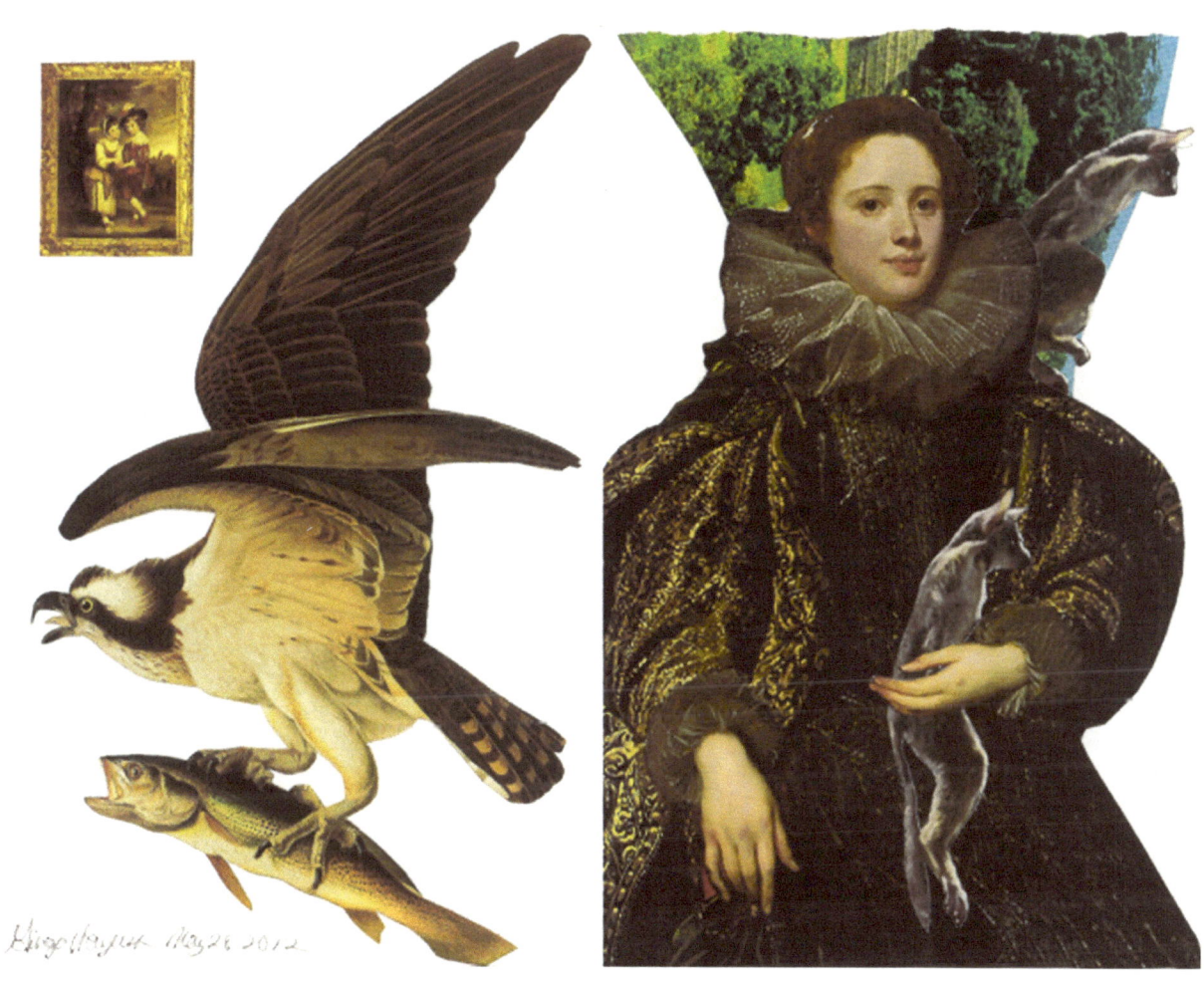

Diptych 9

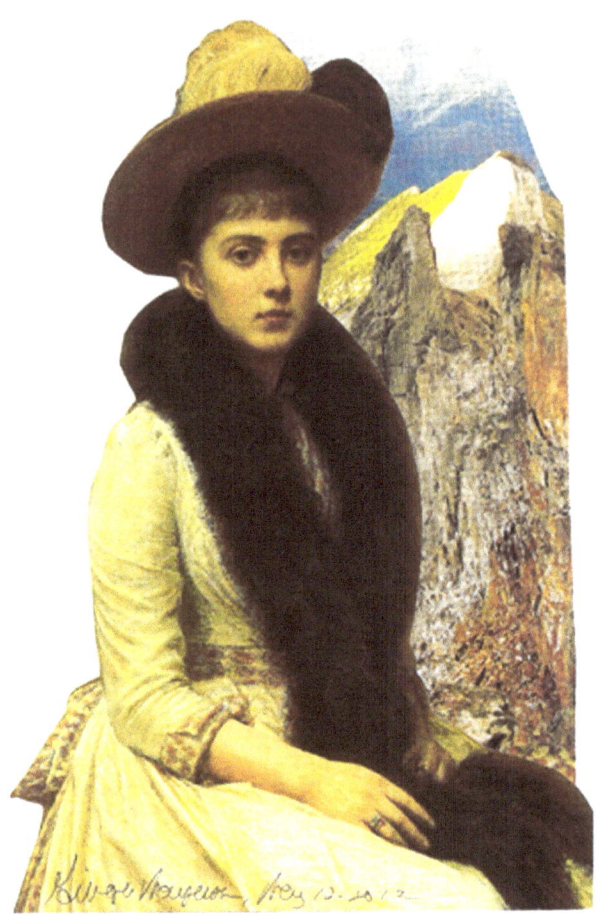 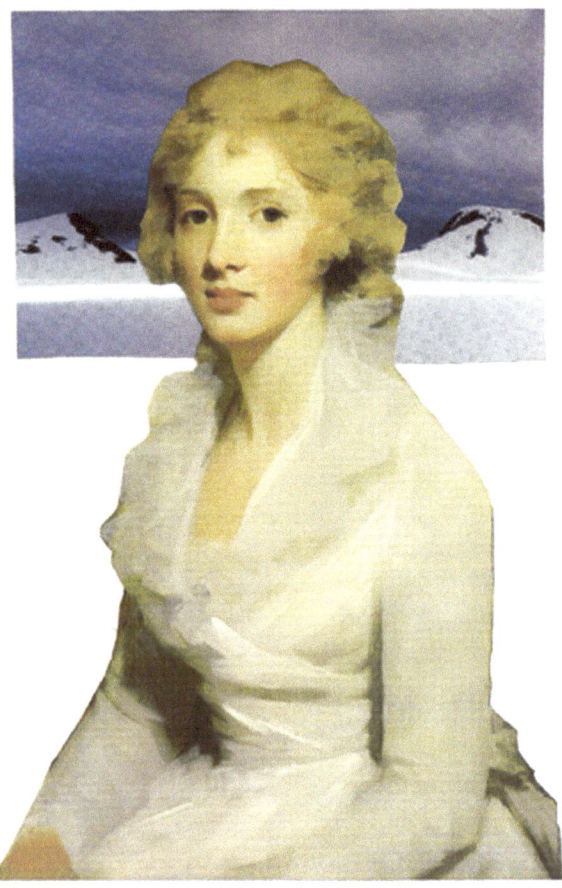

Diptych 10

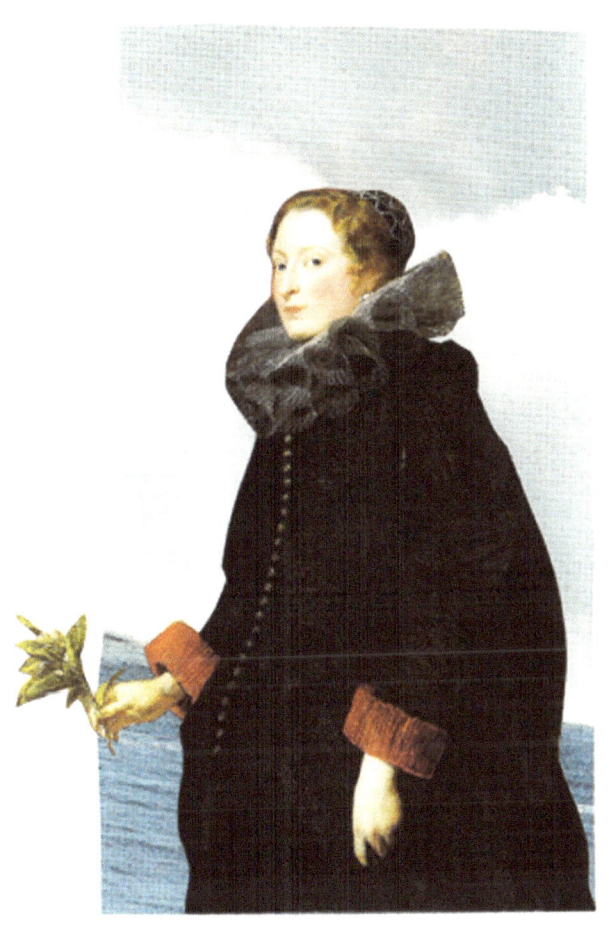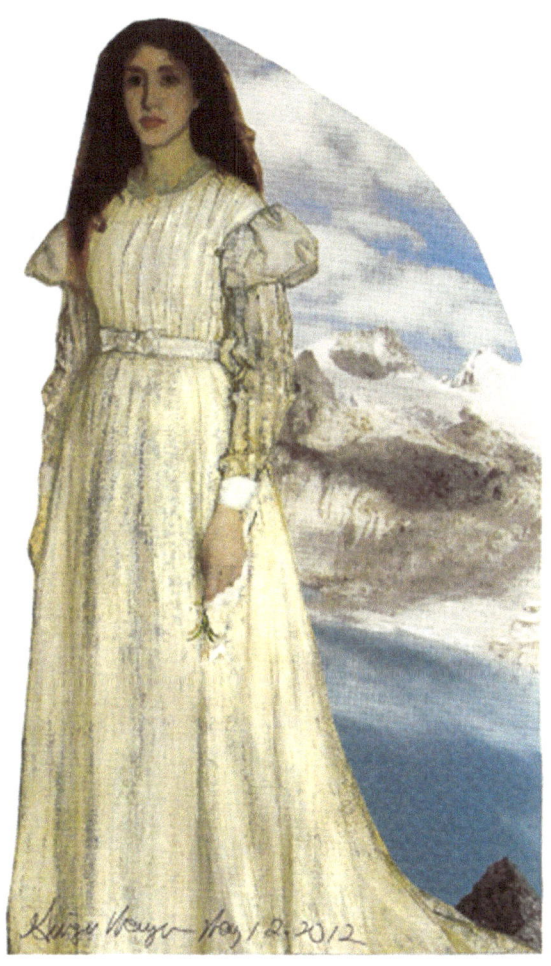

Diptych 11

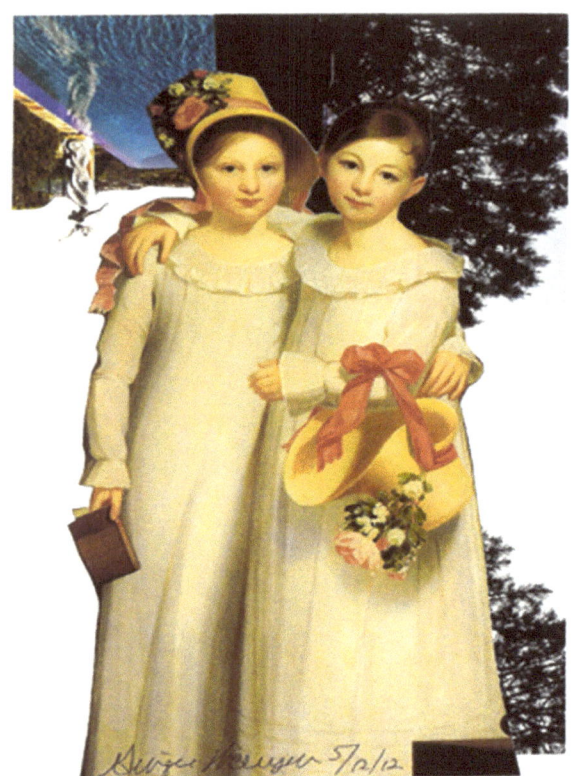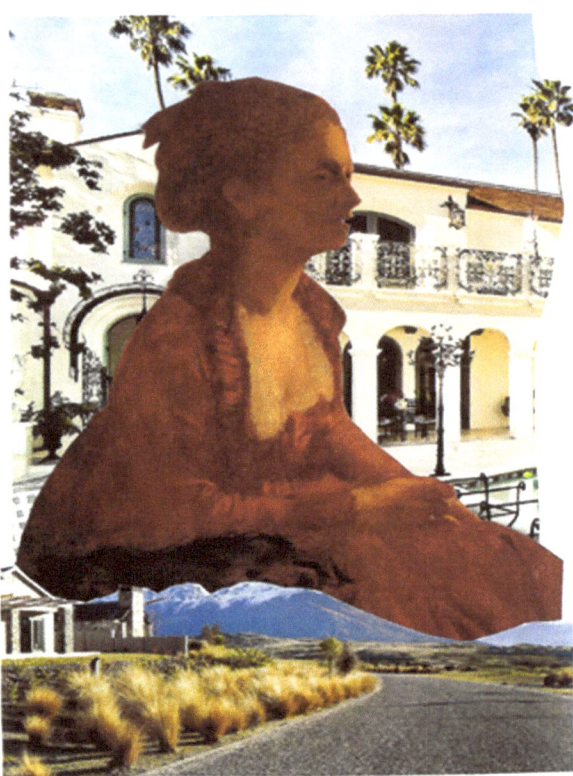

Diptych 12

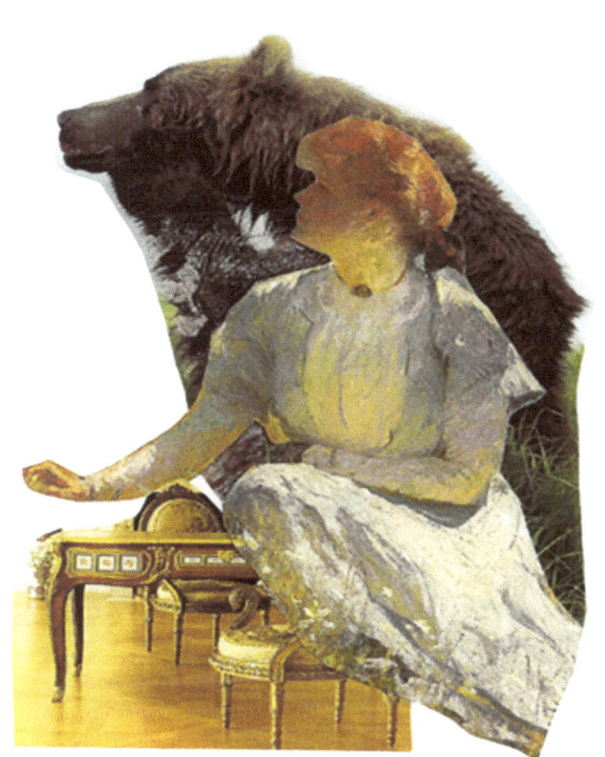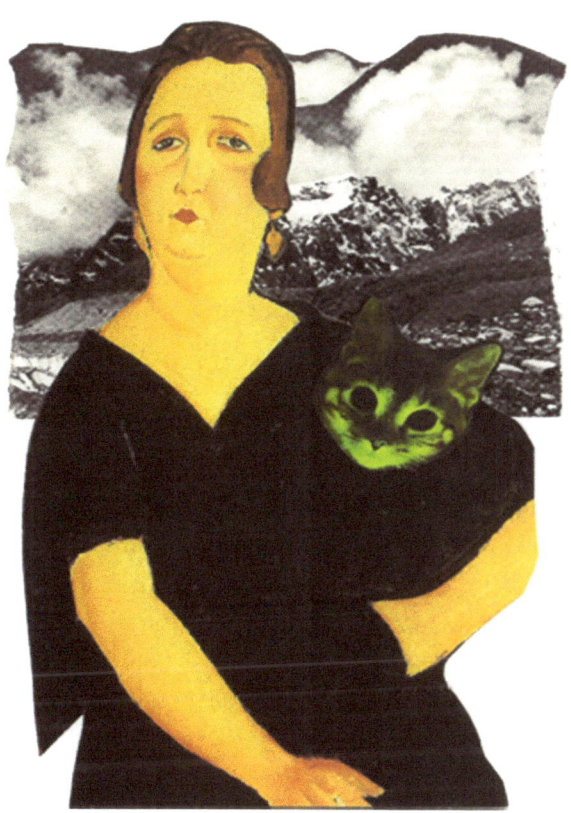

Diptych 13

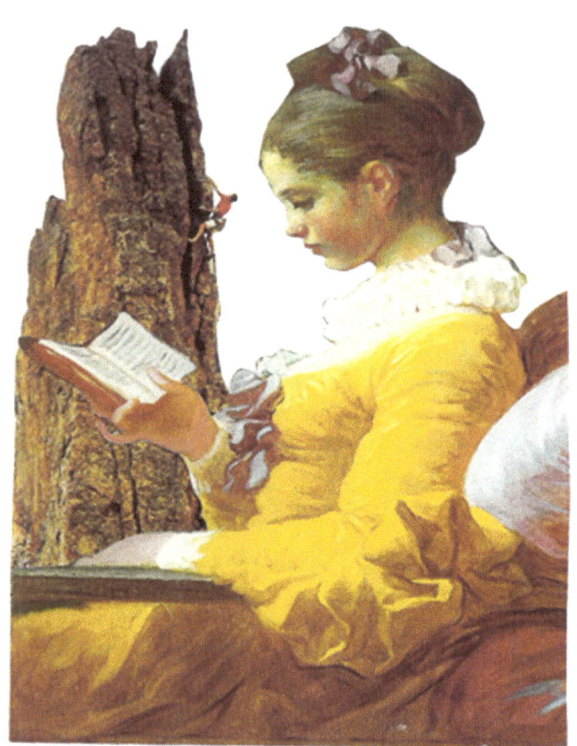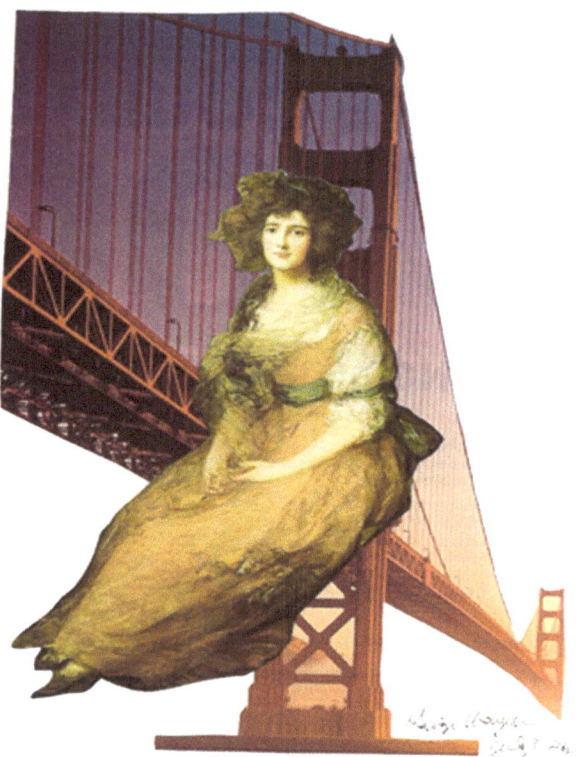

Diptych 14

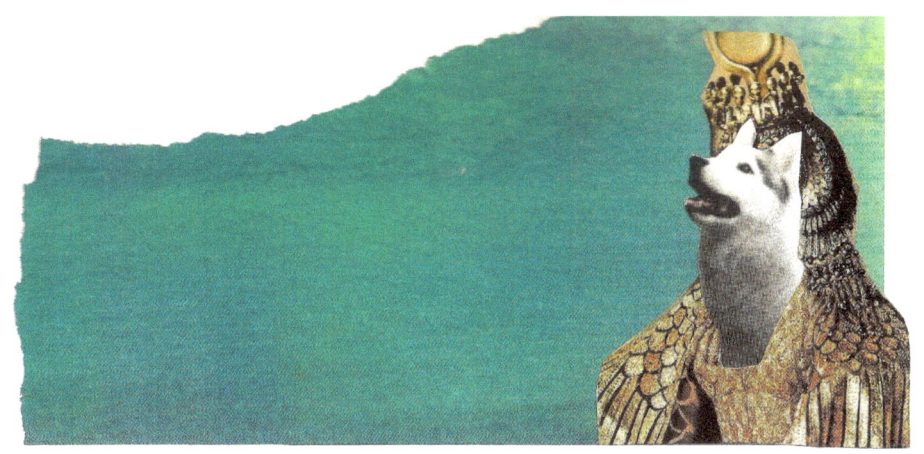
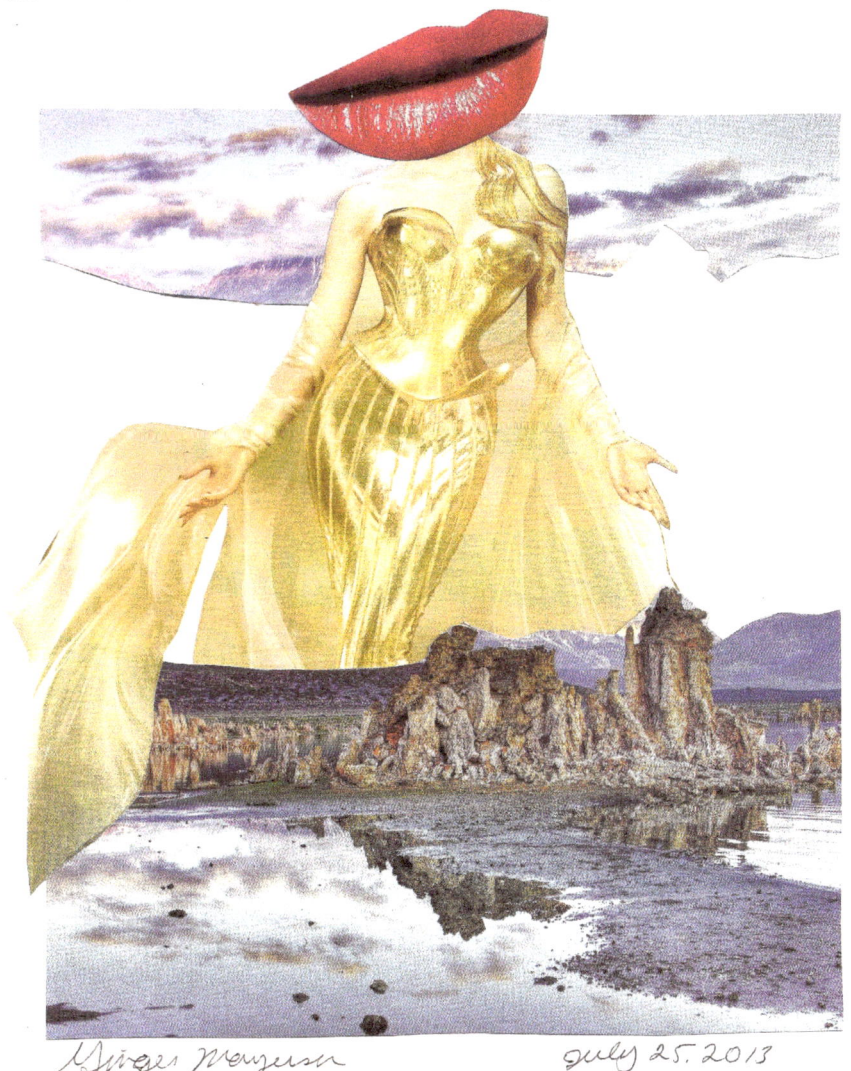

Diptych 15

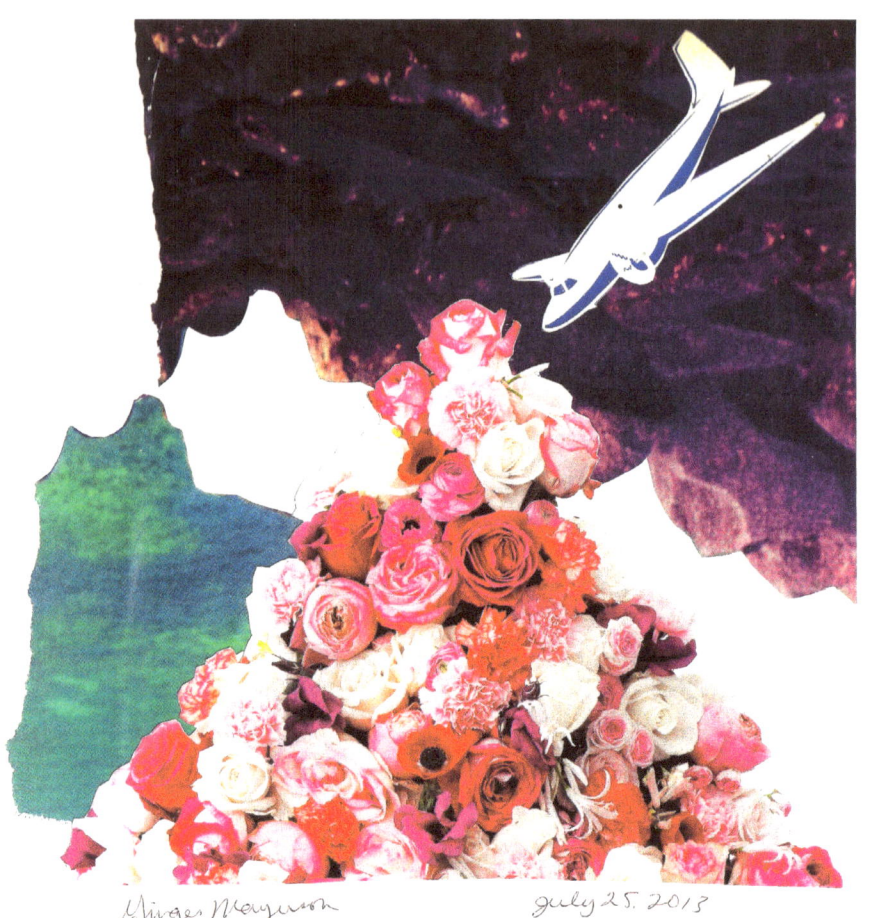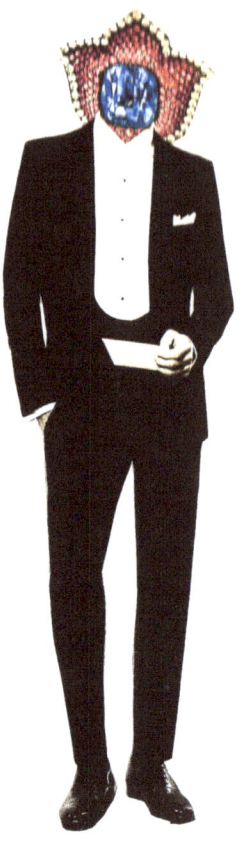

Diptych 16

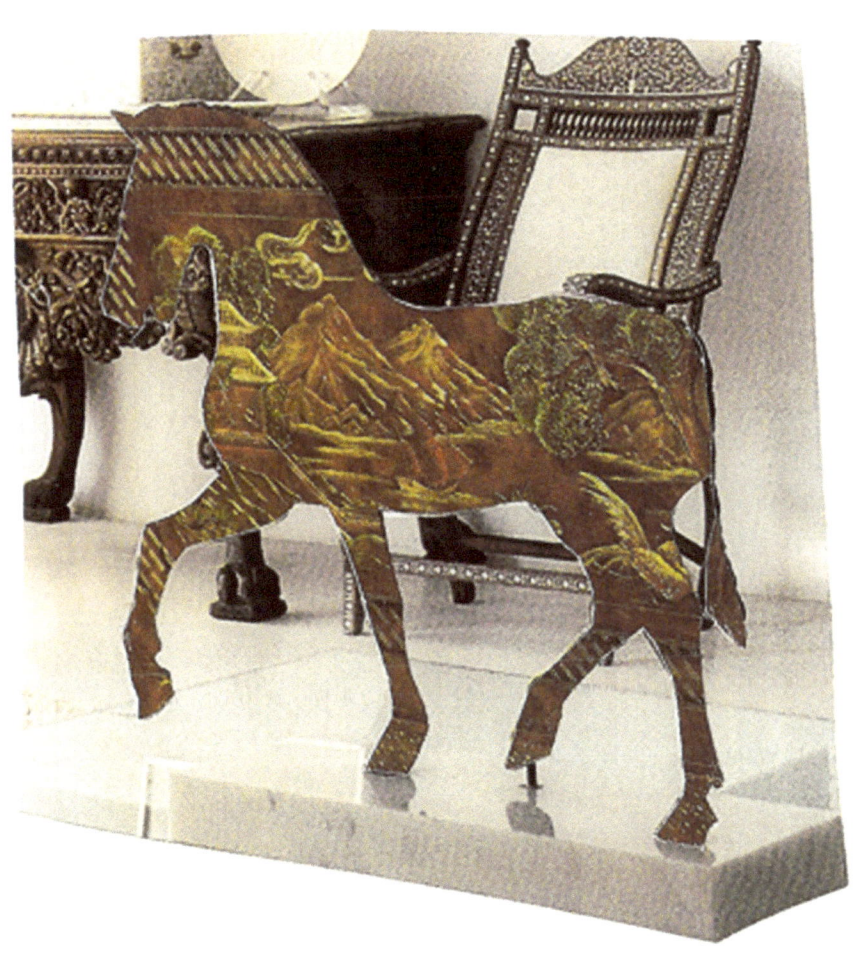

Equestrian, 5.5x5.5"

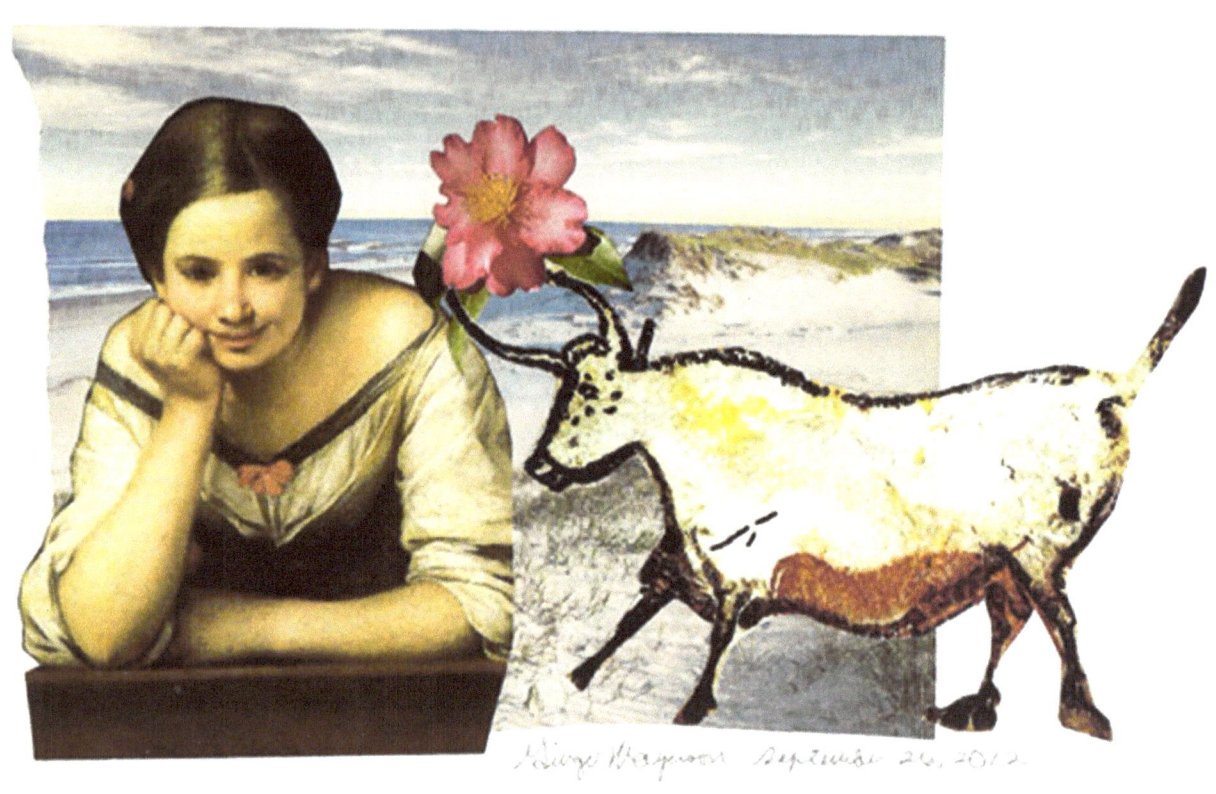

Europa-a-Go-Go, 7x10"

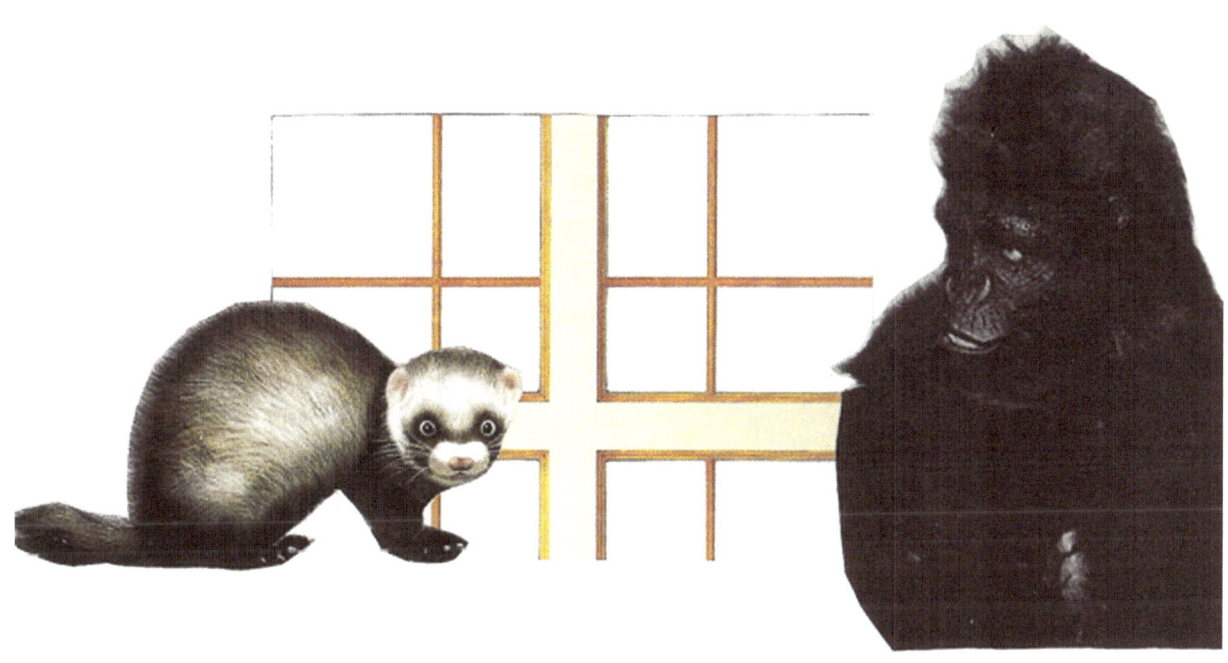

Ferret Romance, 4x6"

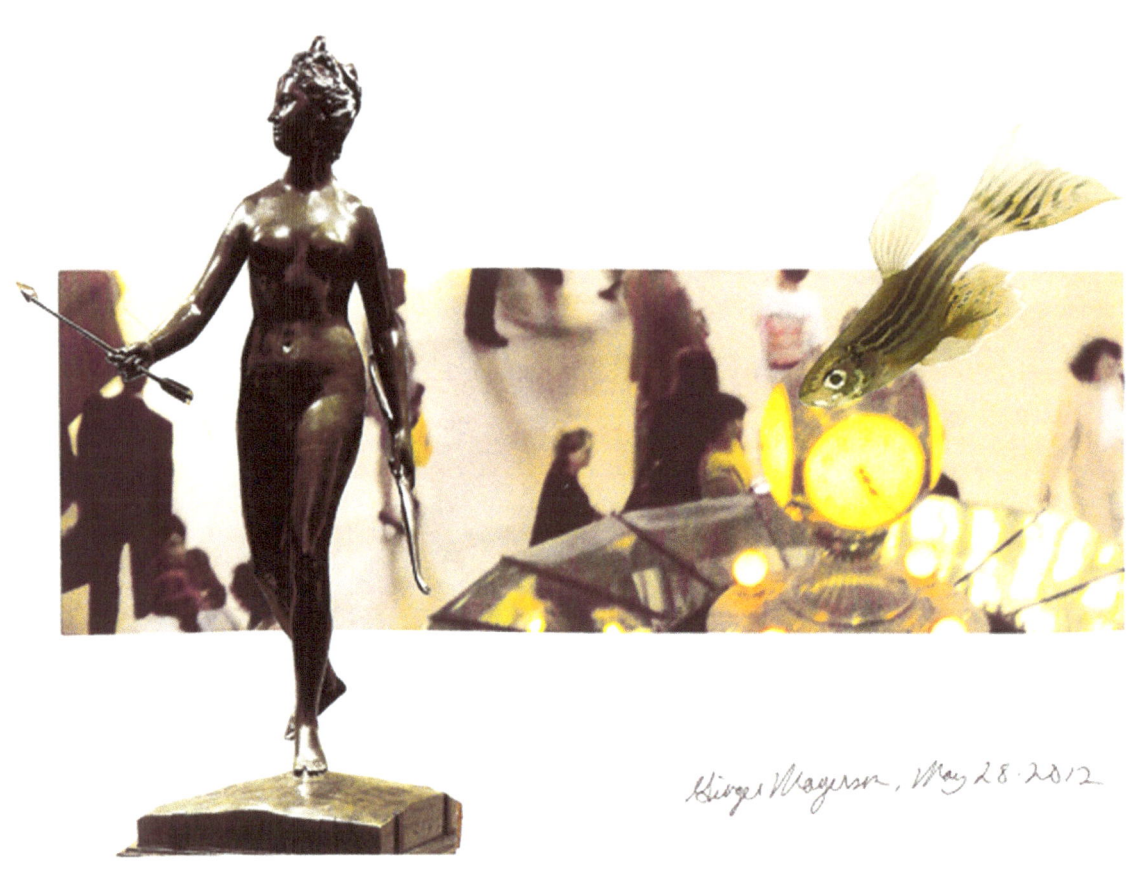

Fish Tank, 7x10"

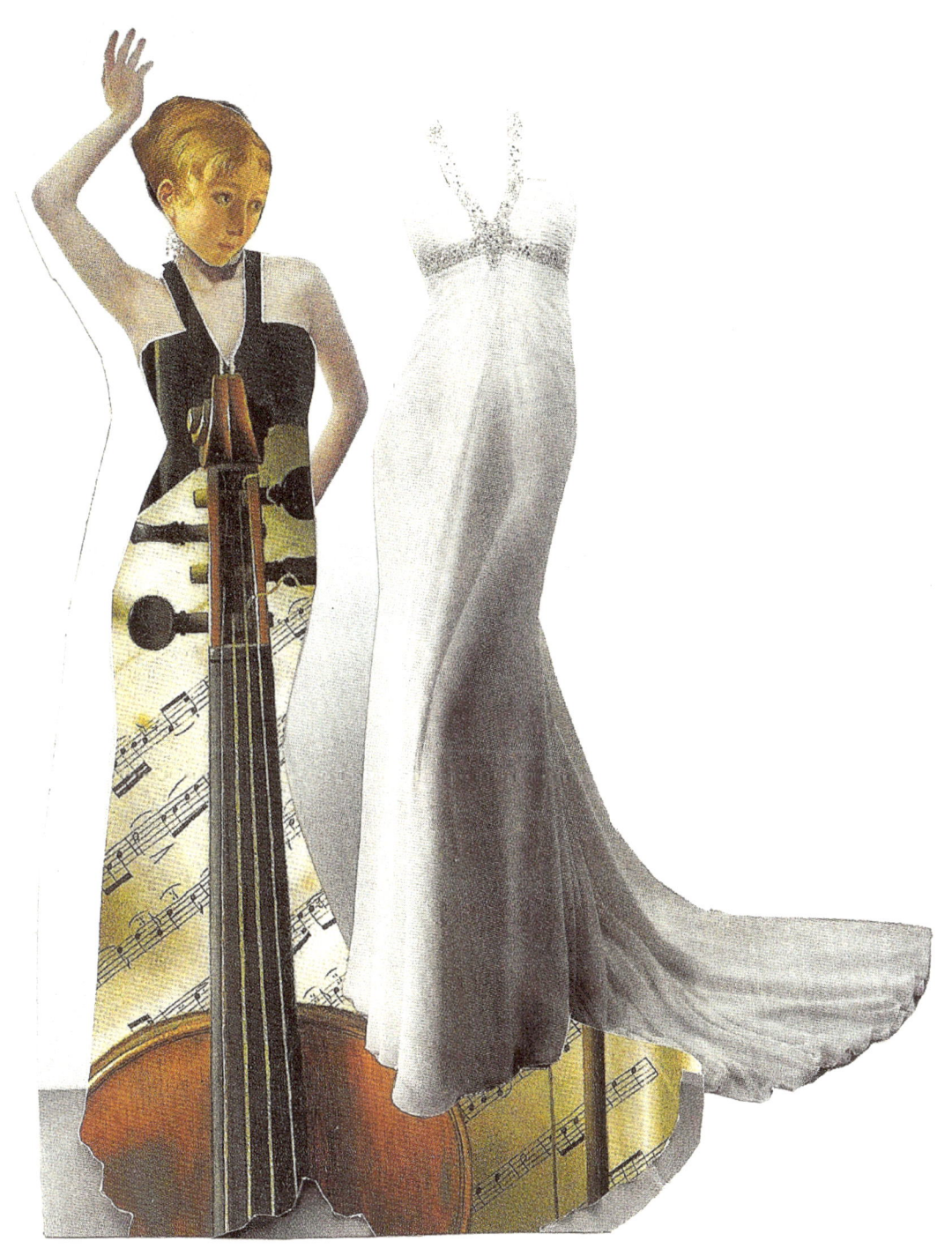

Fiddle Dress, 6x4"

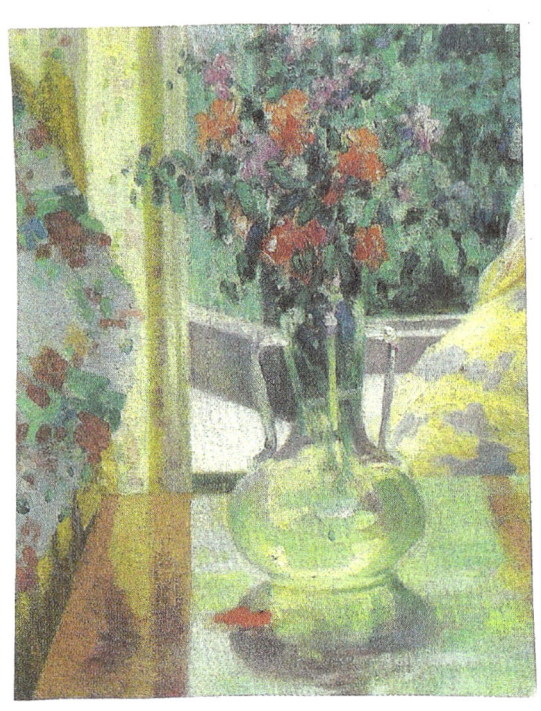 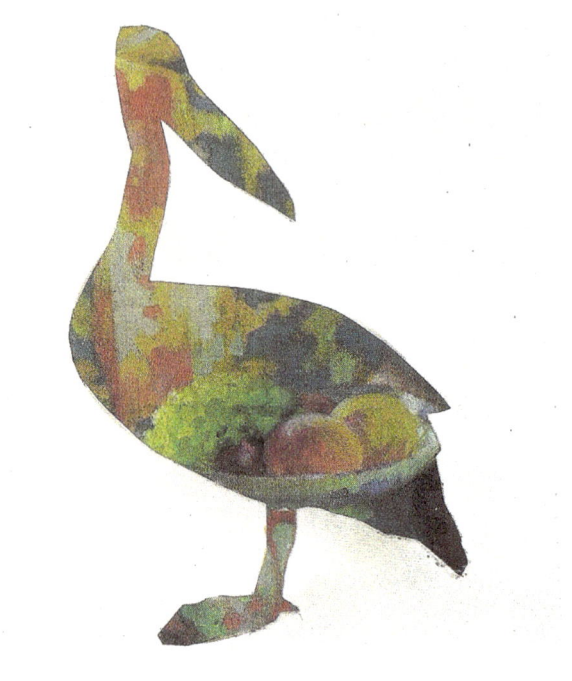

Floral Bird, 4x6"

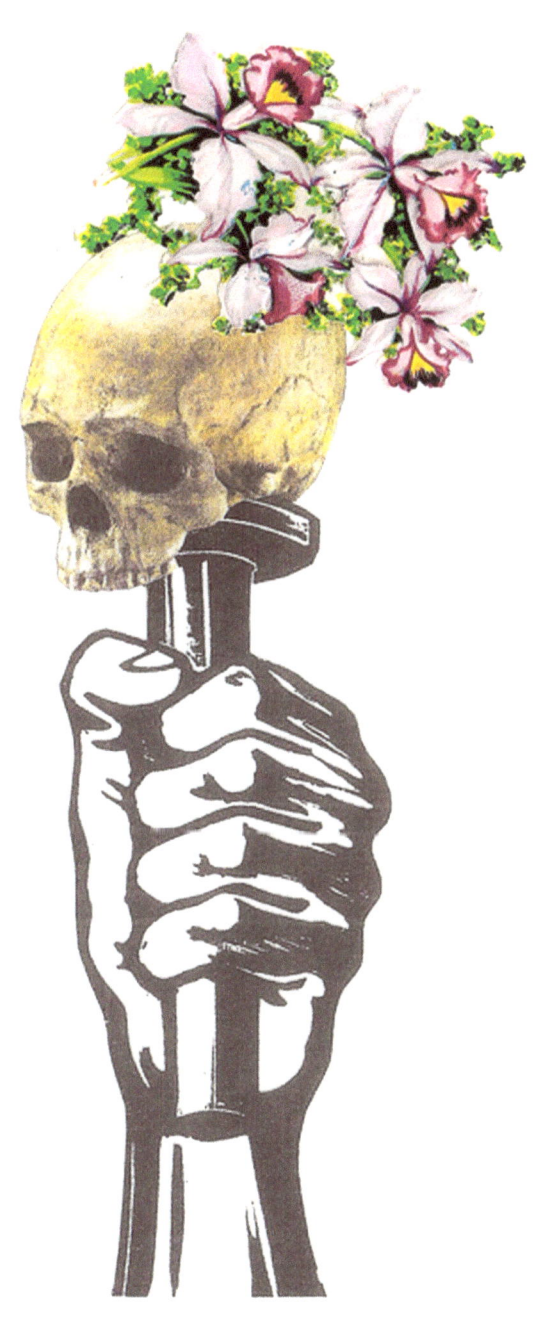

Floral Stand, 6x4"

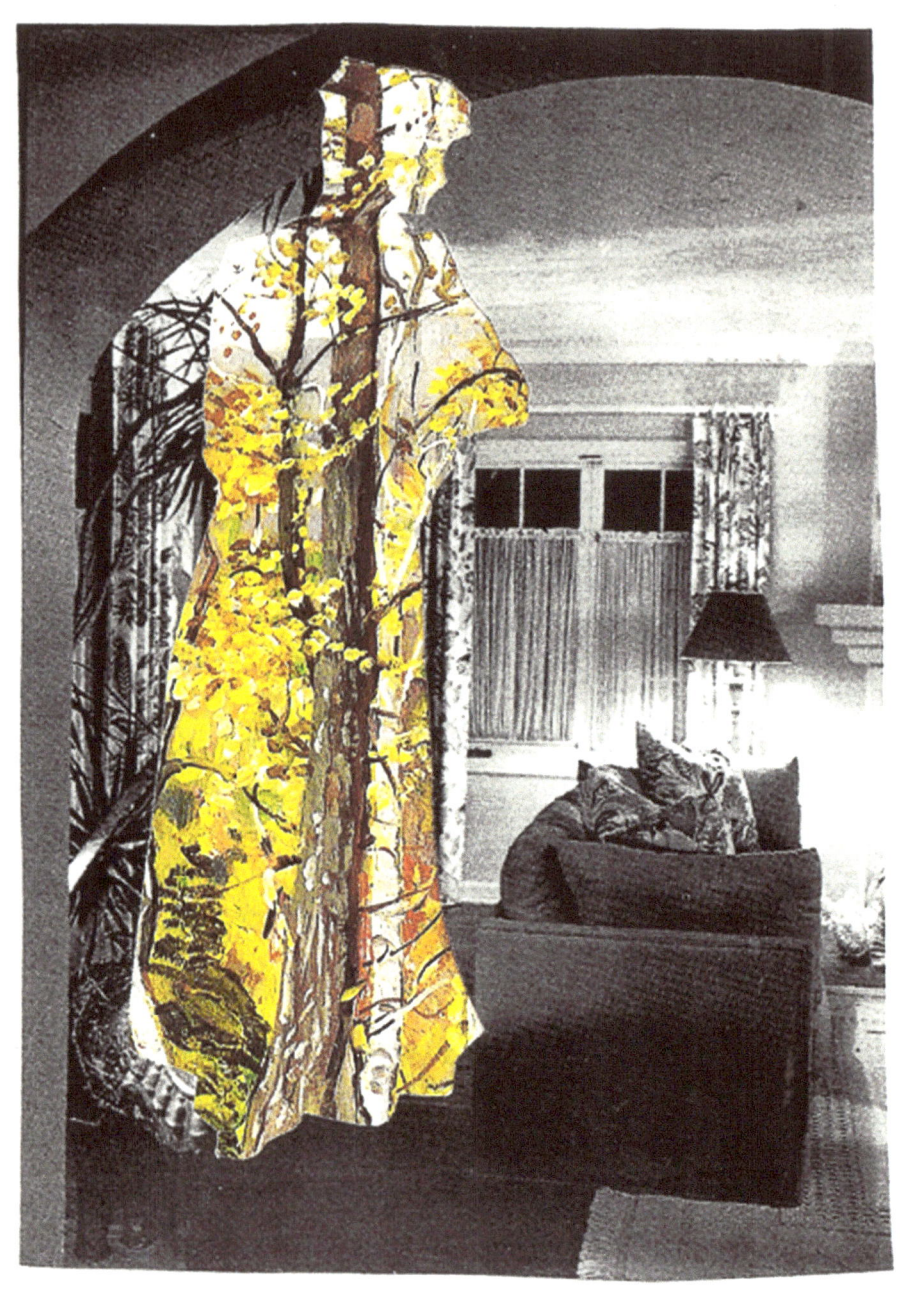

Forest, 6x4"

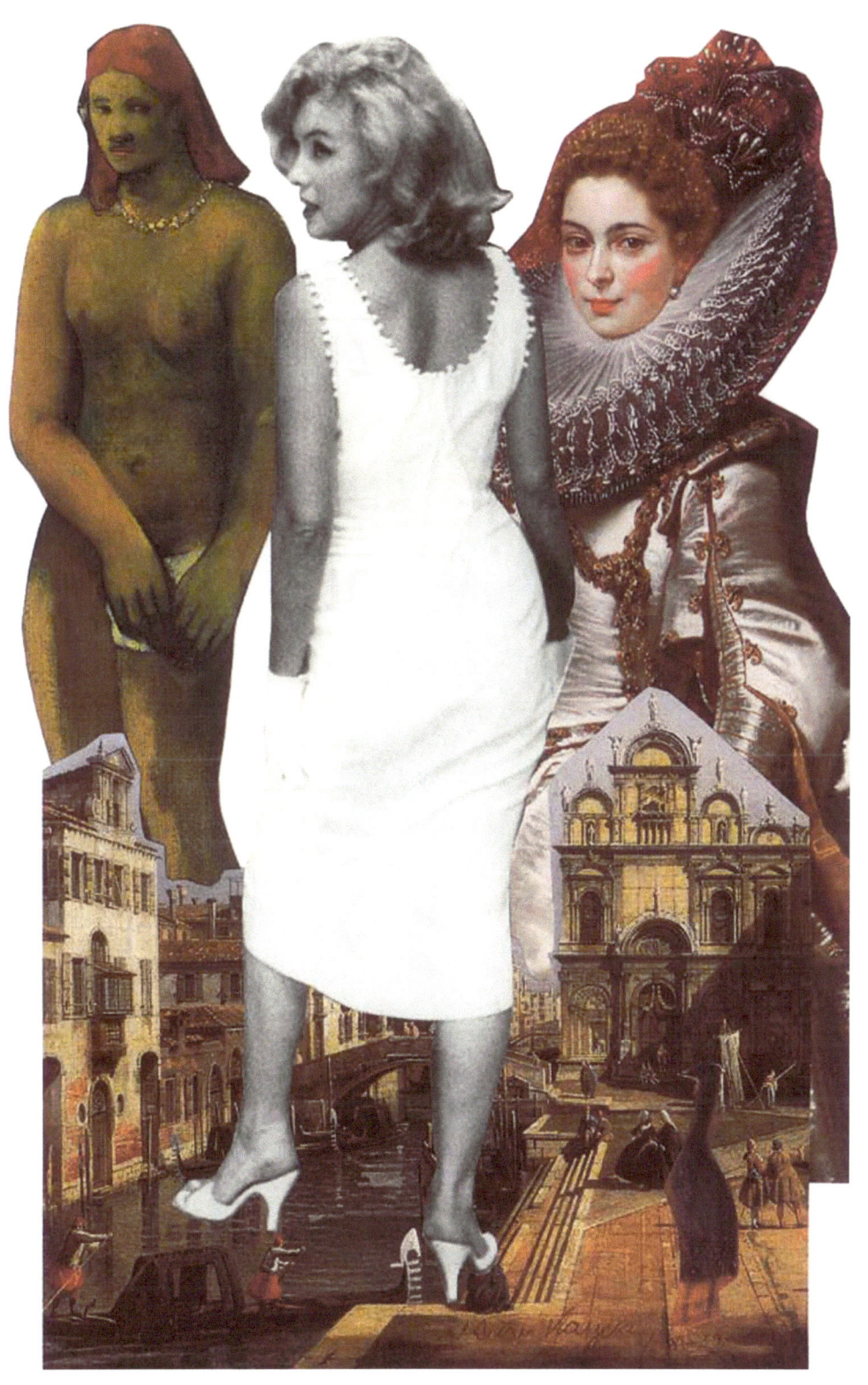

Girlfriends 2, 10x7"

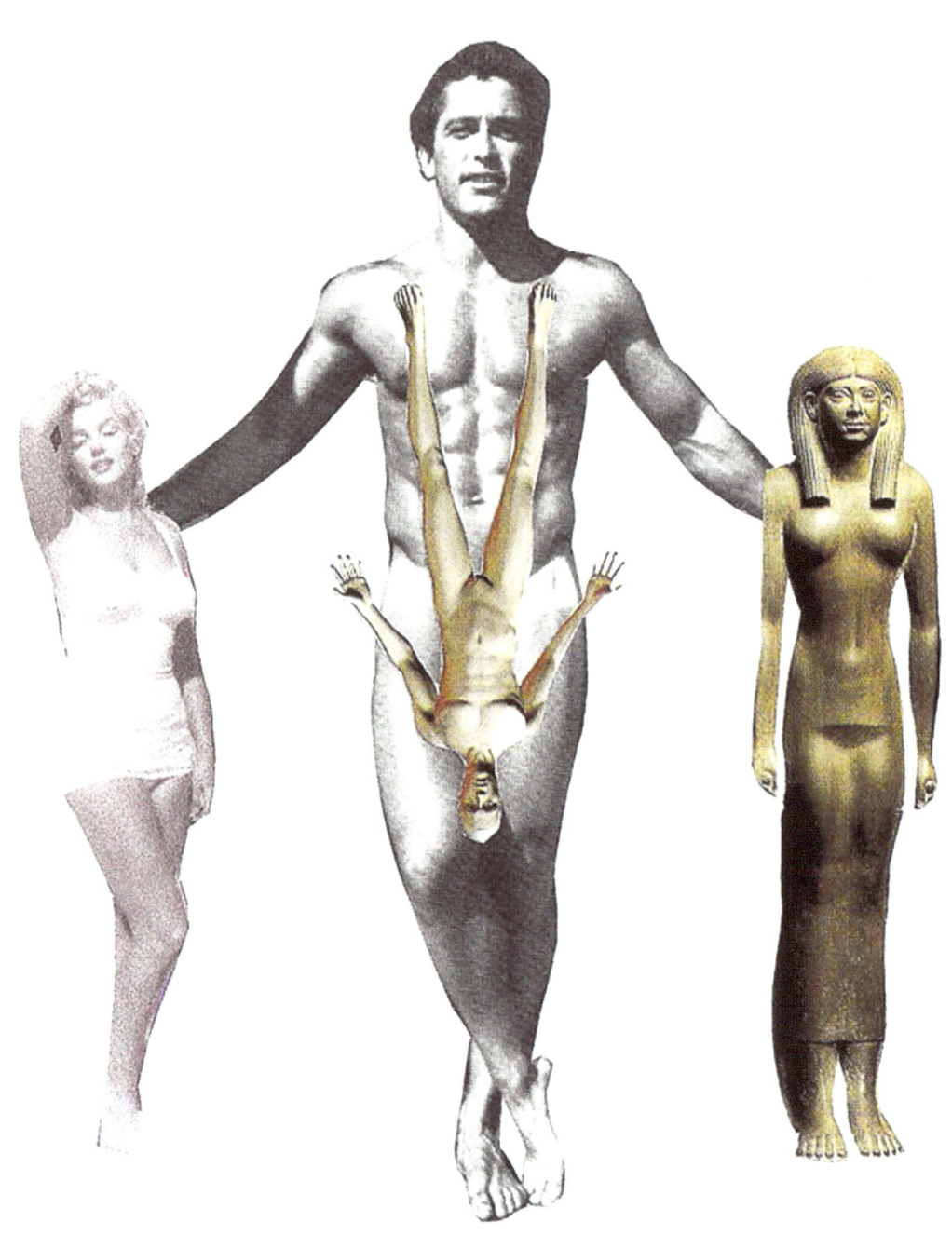

Girls, Girls, 6x4"

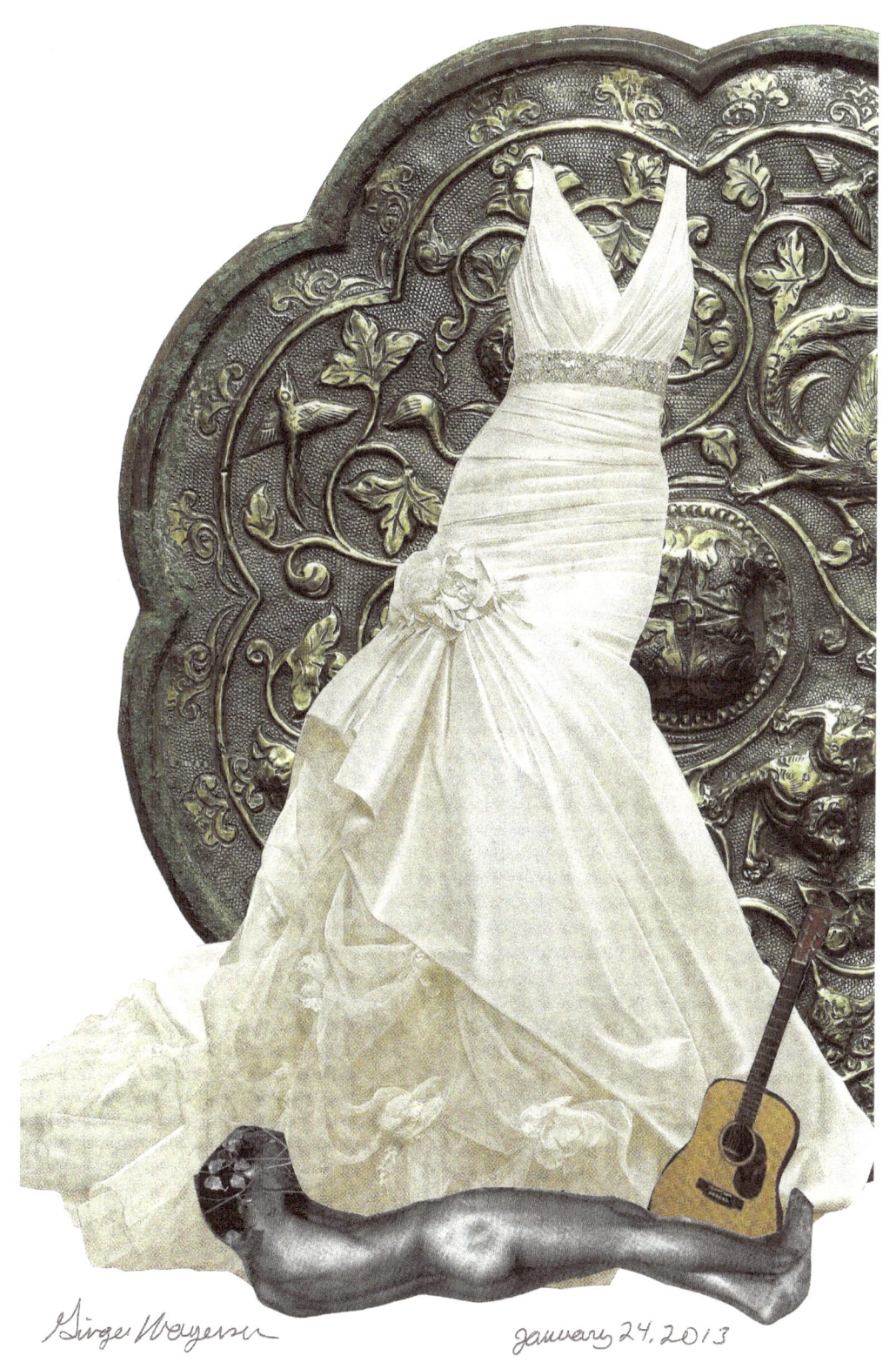

Guitar Bride, 10x7"

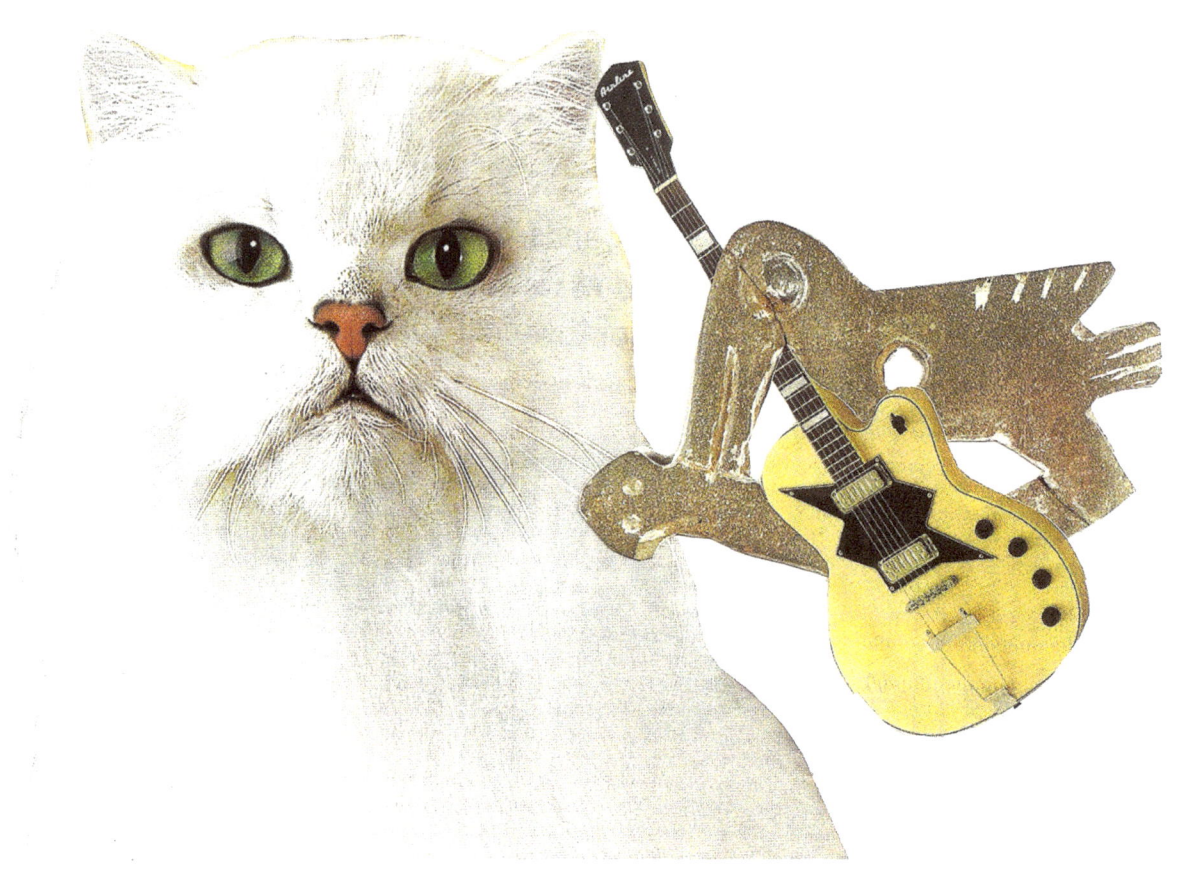

Guitar Cat, 4x6"

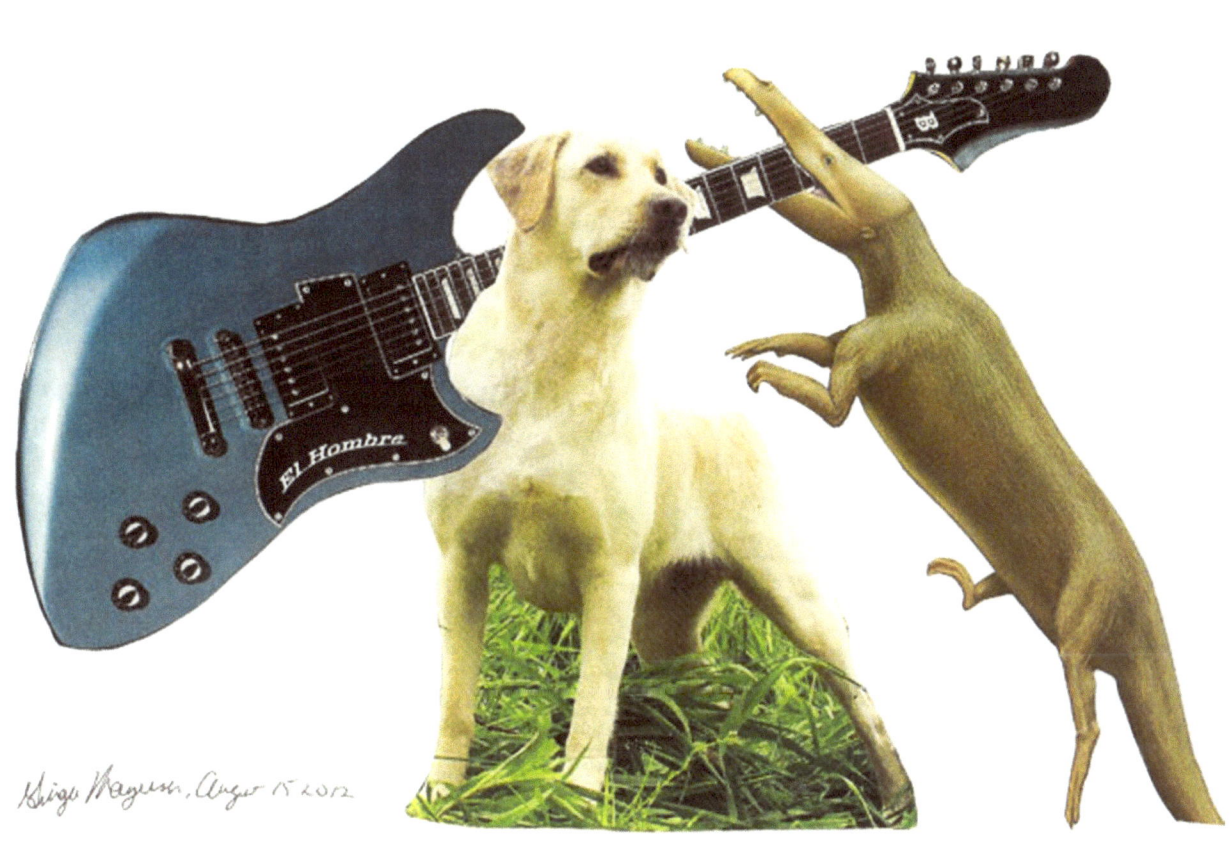

Guitar Dog, 7x10"

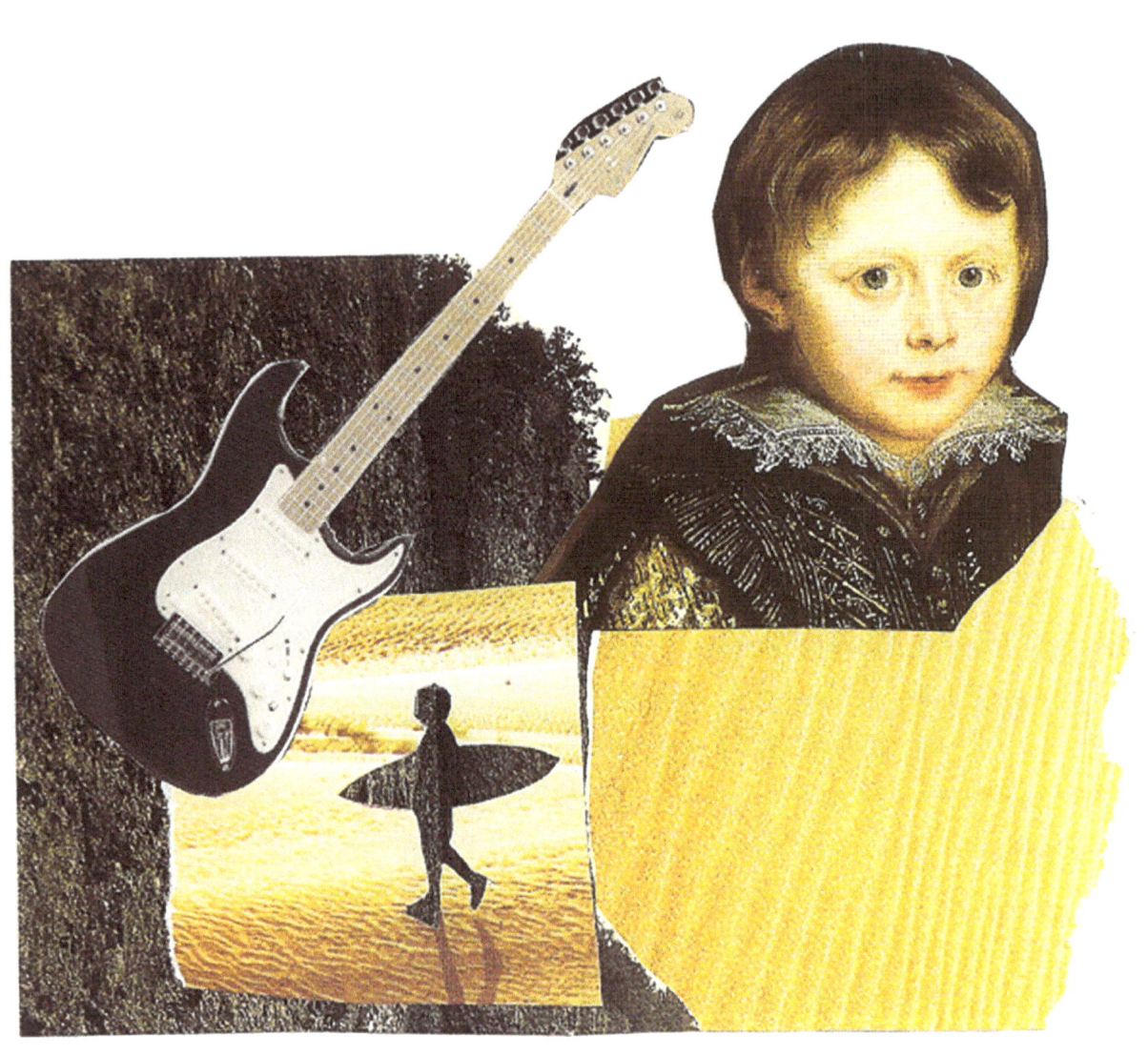

Guitar Kid, 5.5x5.5"

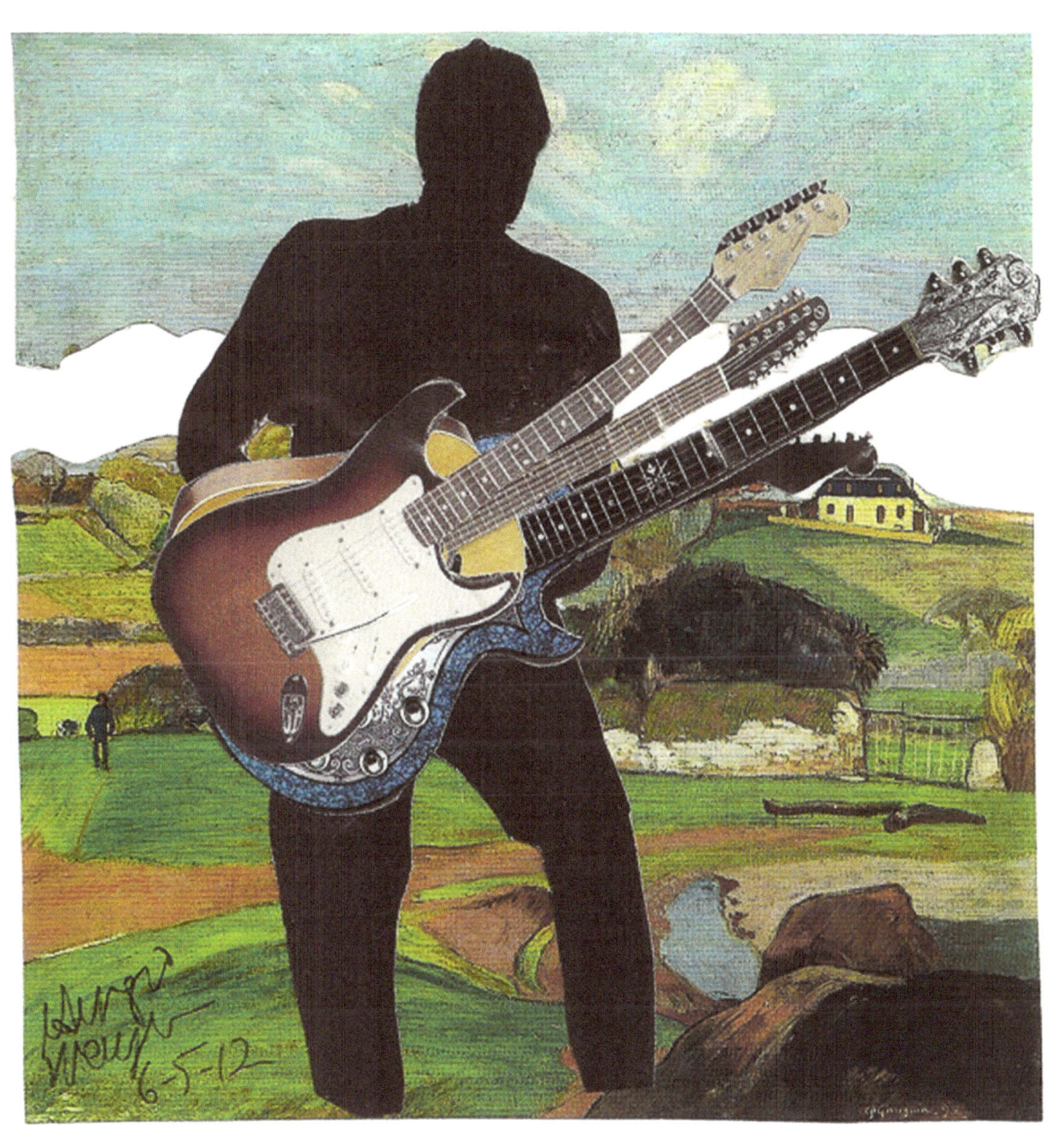

Guitars Man, 5.5x5.5"

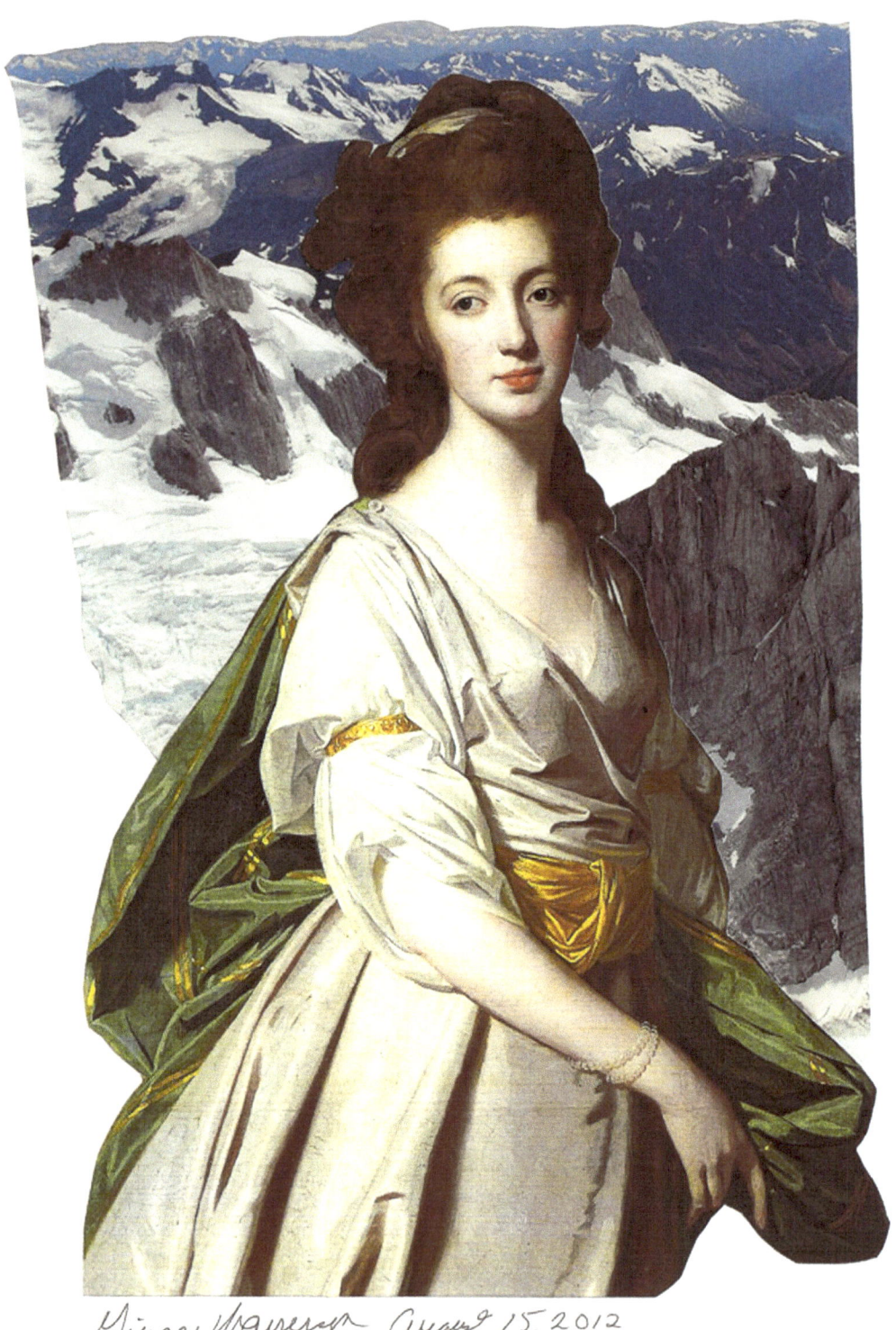

Lady of the Mountains, 10x7"

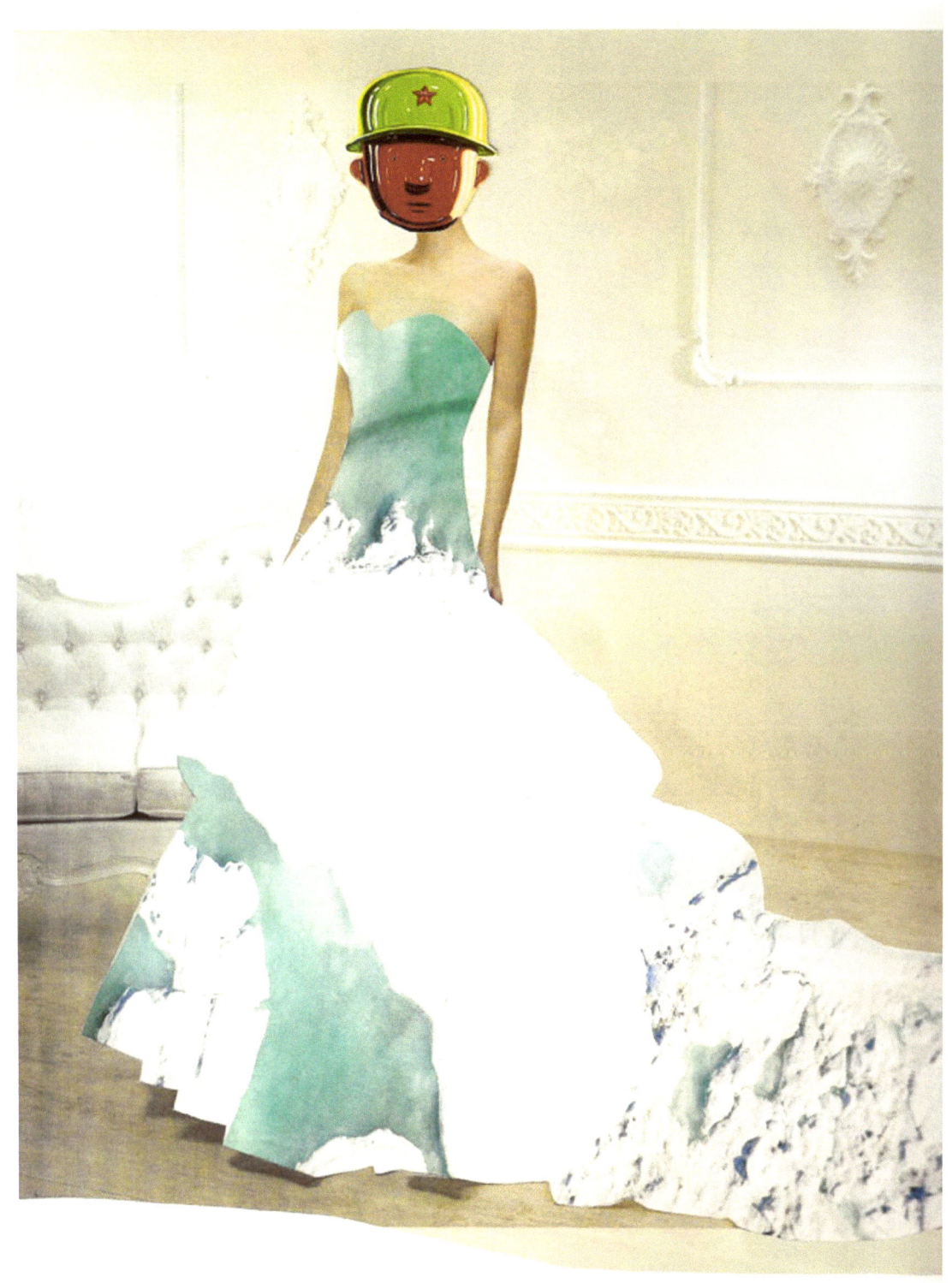

Ice Dress, 12x9"

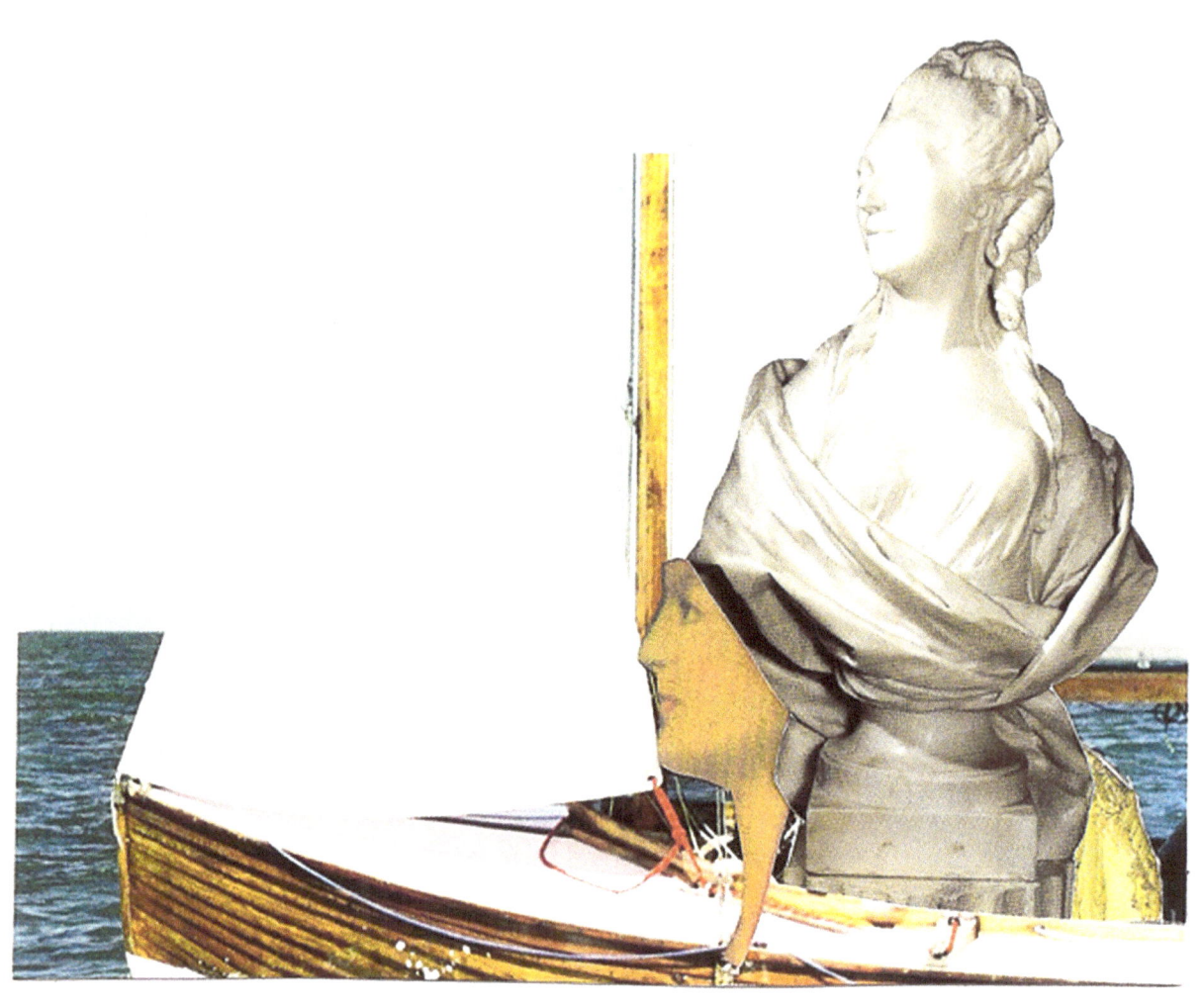

Land Ho, 5.5x5.5"

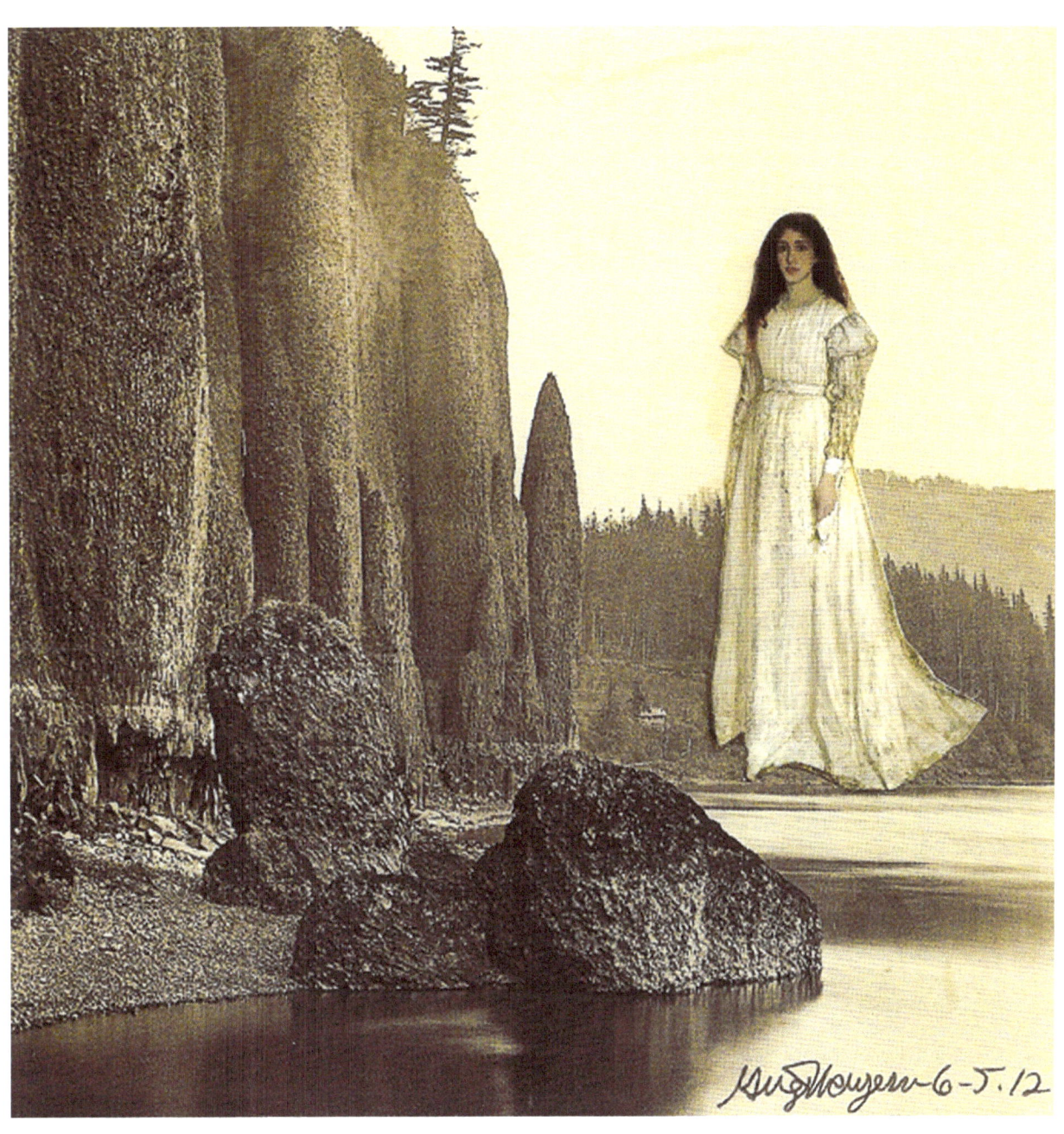

Lake Lady, 5.5x5.5"

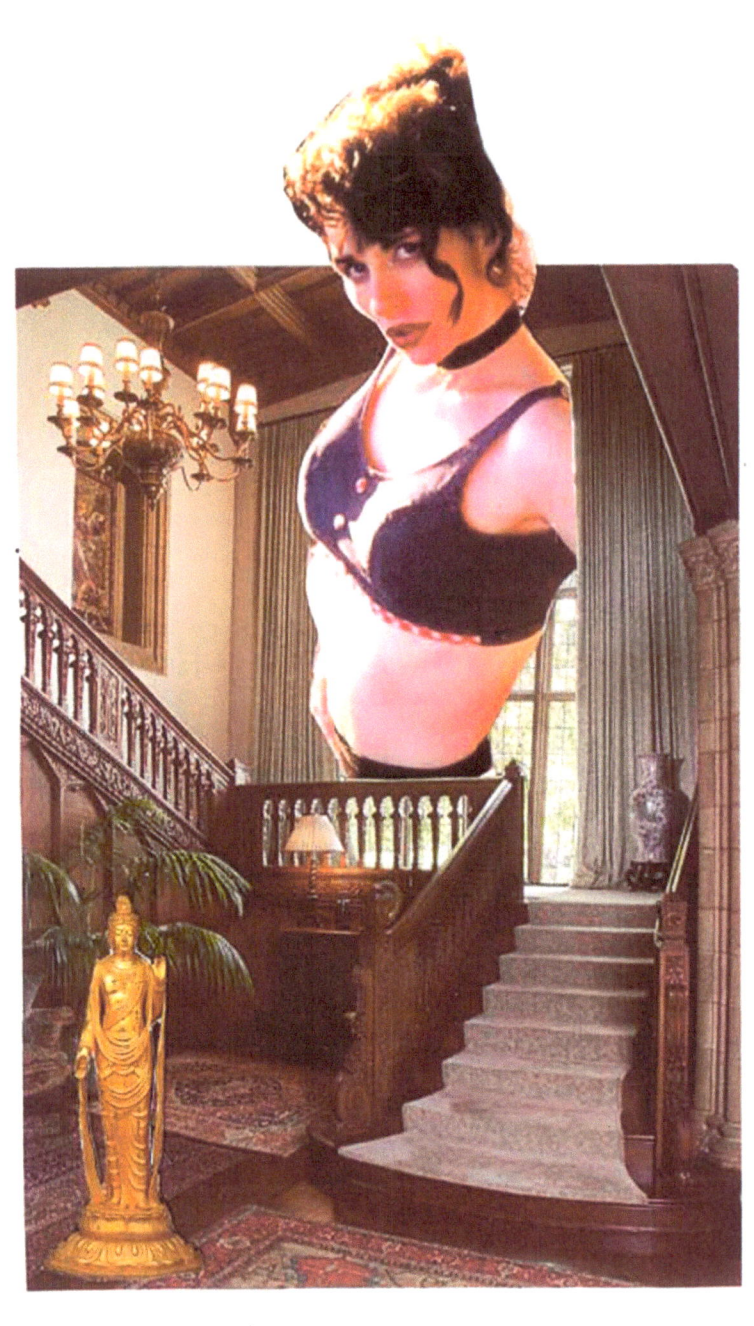

Melanie Marie Brown, 6x4"

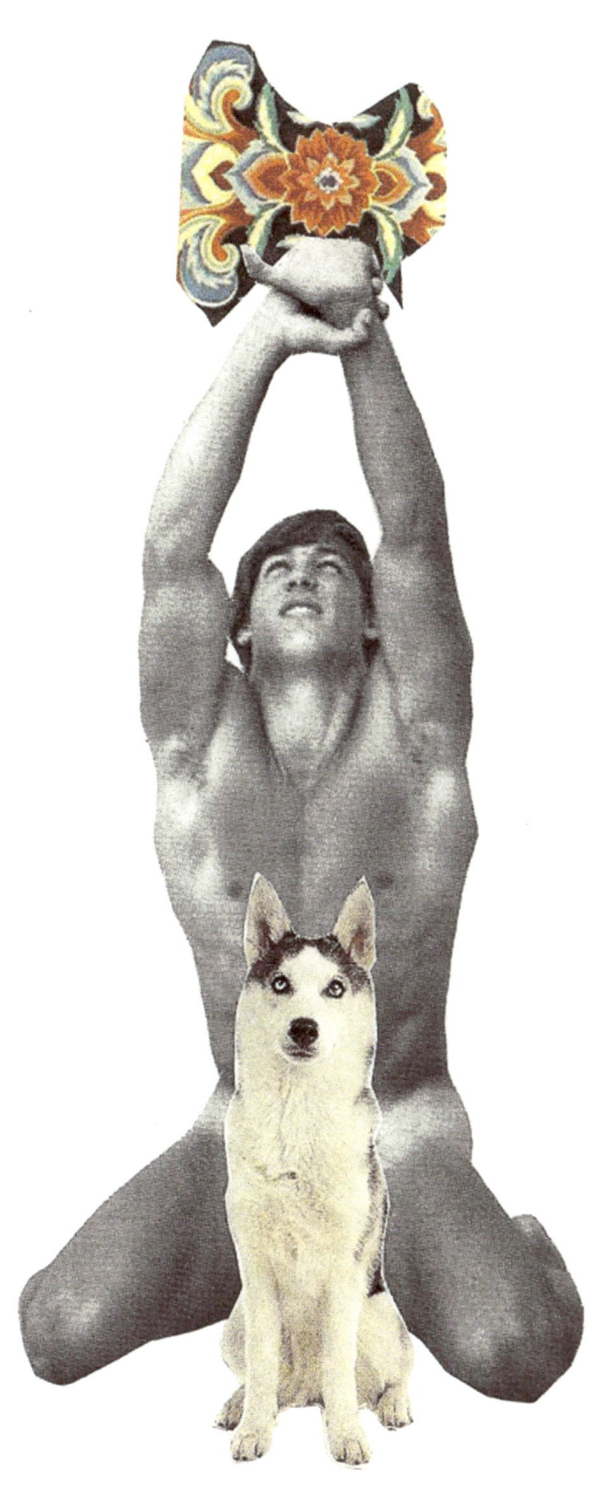

Man's Best Friend, 6x4"

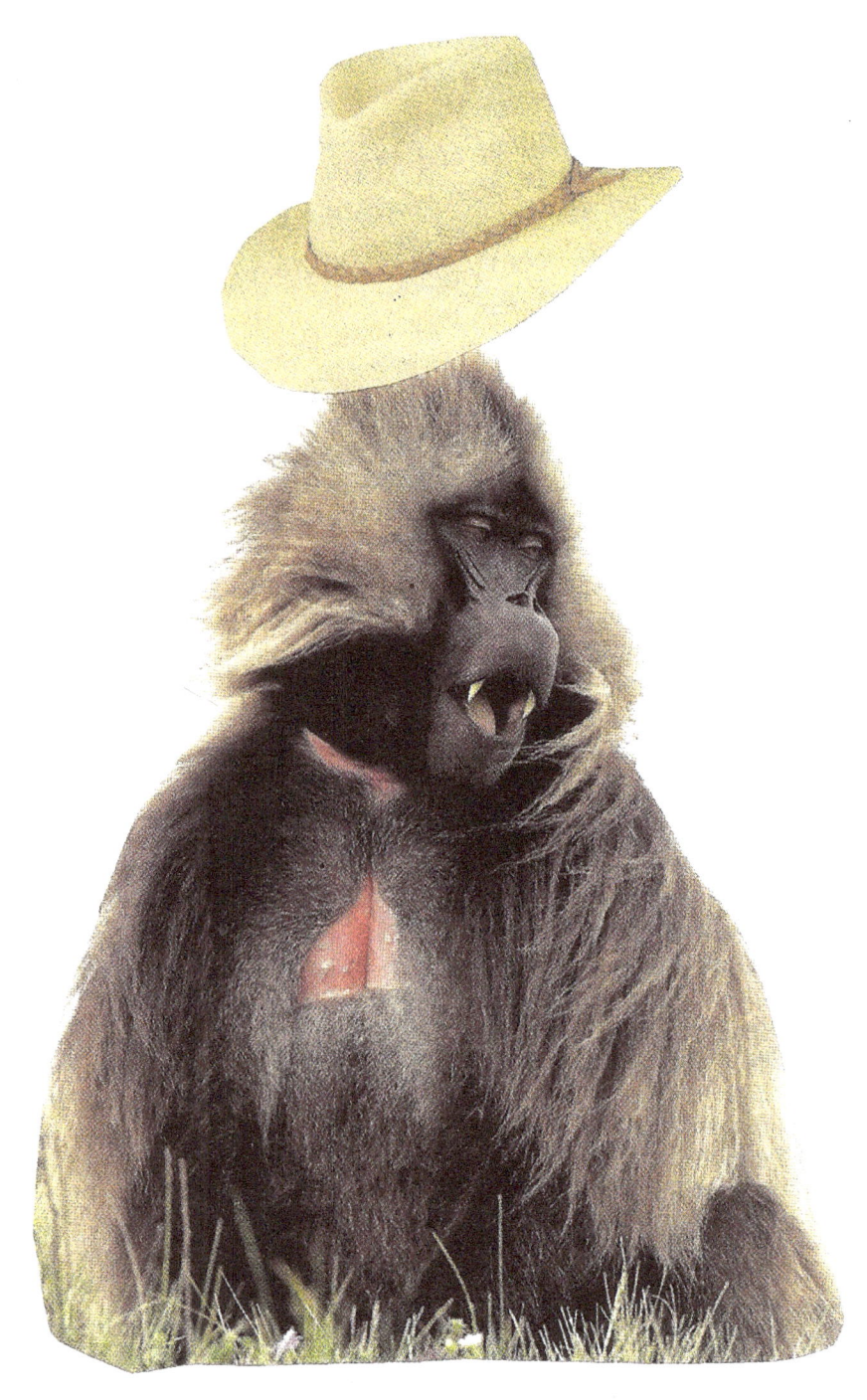

Monkey Hat, 6x4"

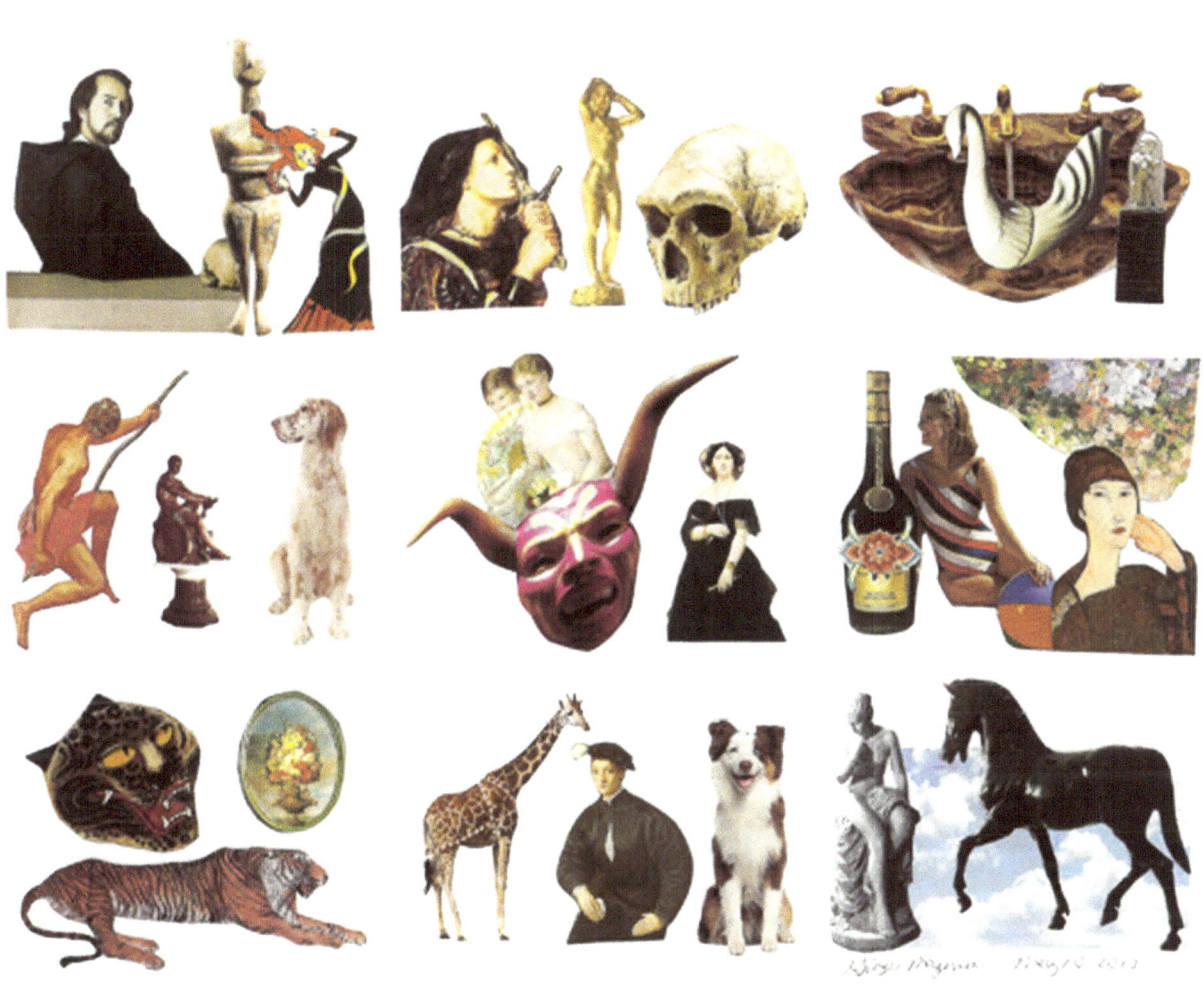

Nonette, 9x12"

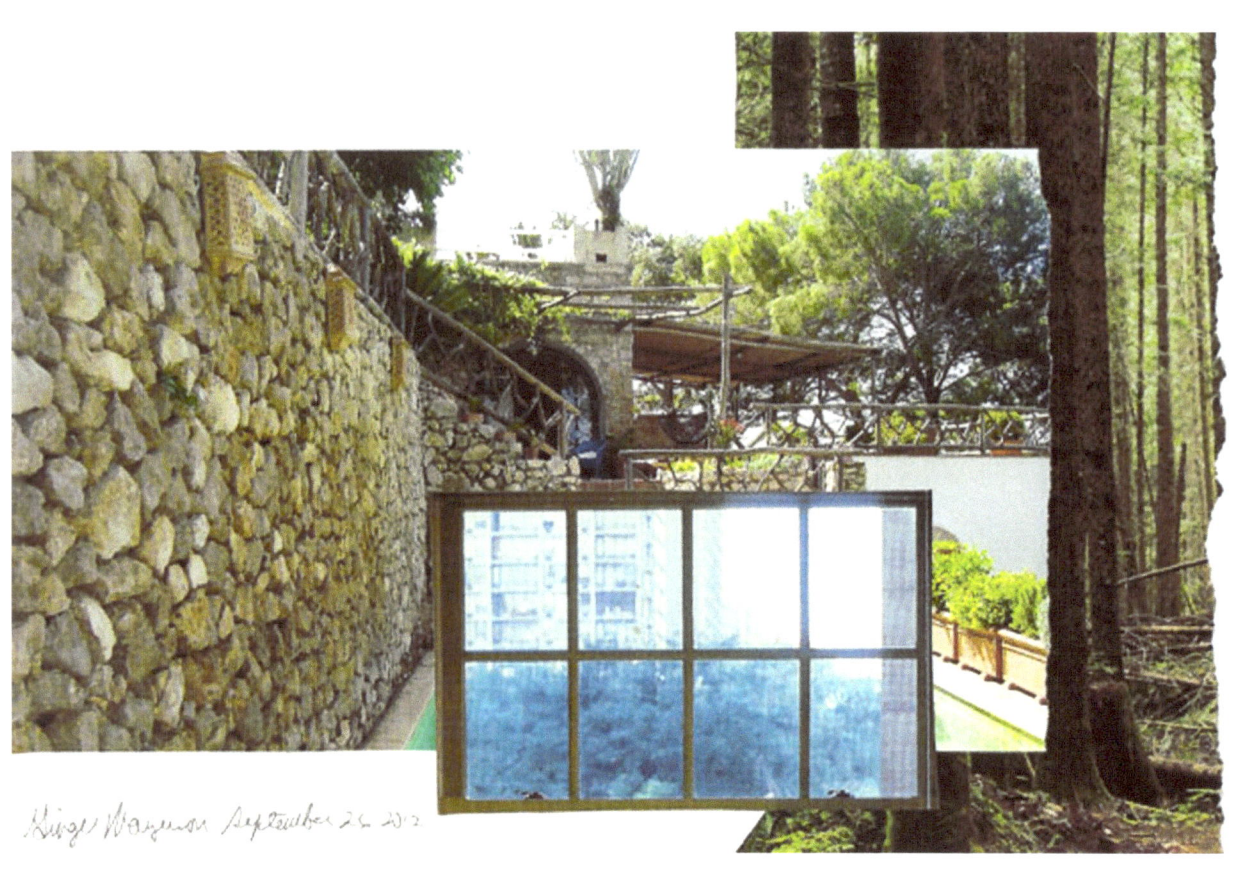

Pool View, 7x10"

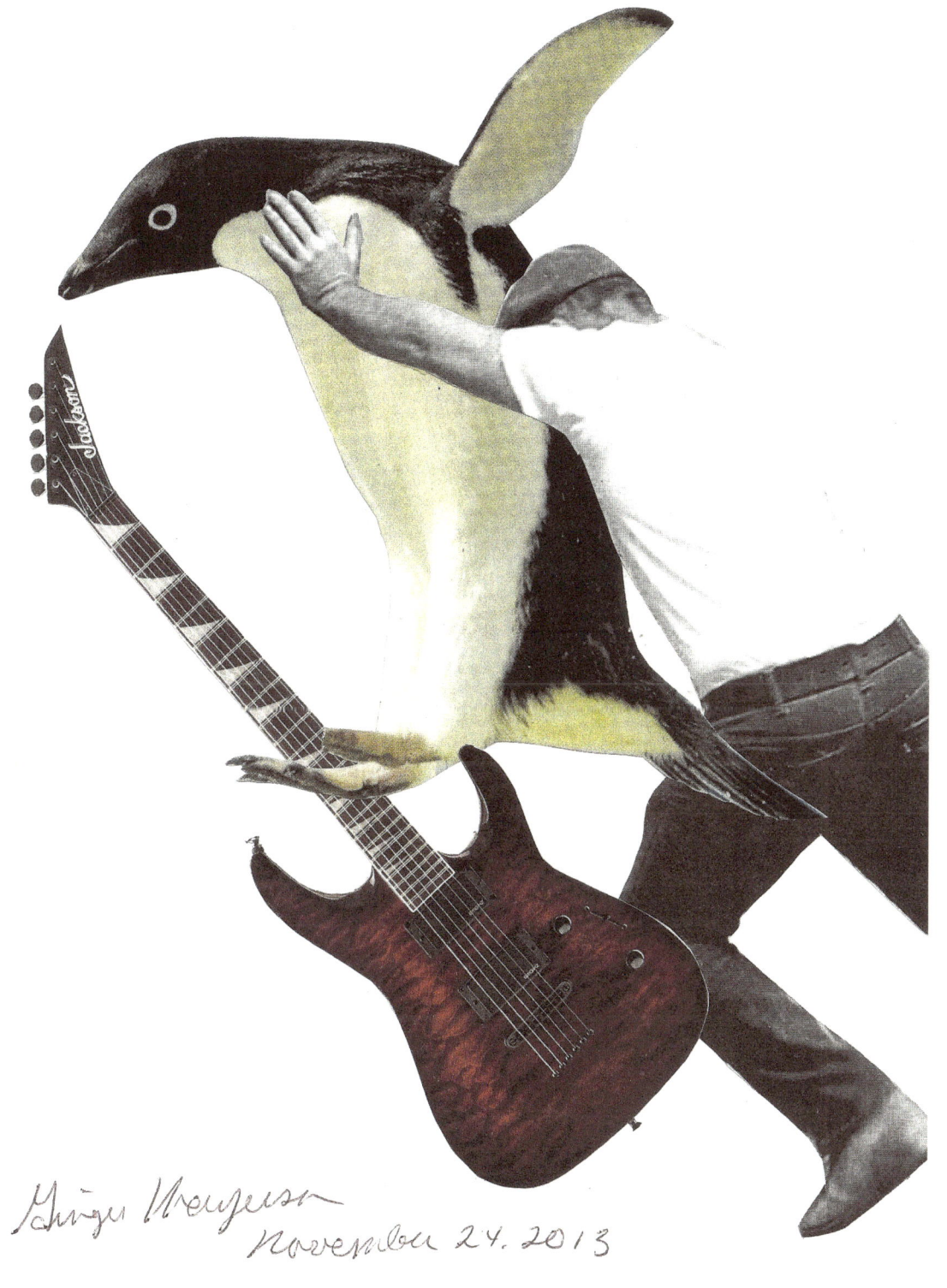

Penguin Guitar, 8x5.5"

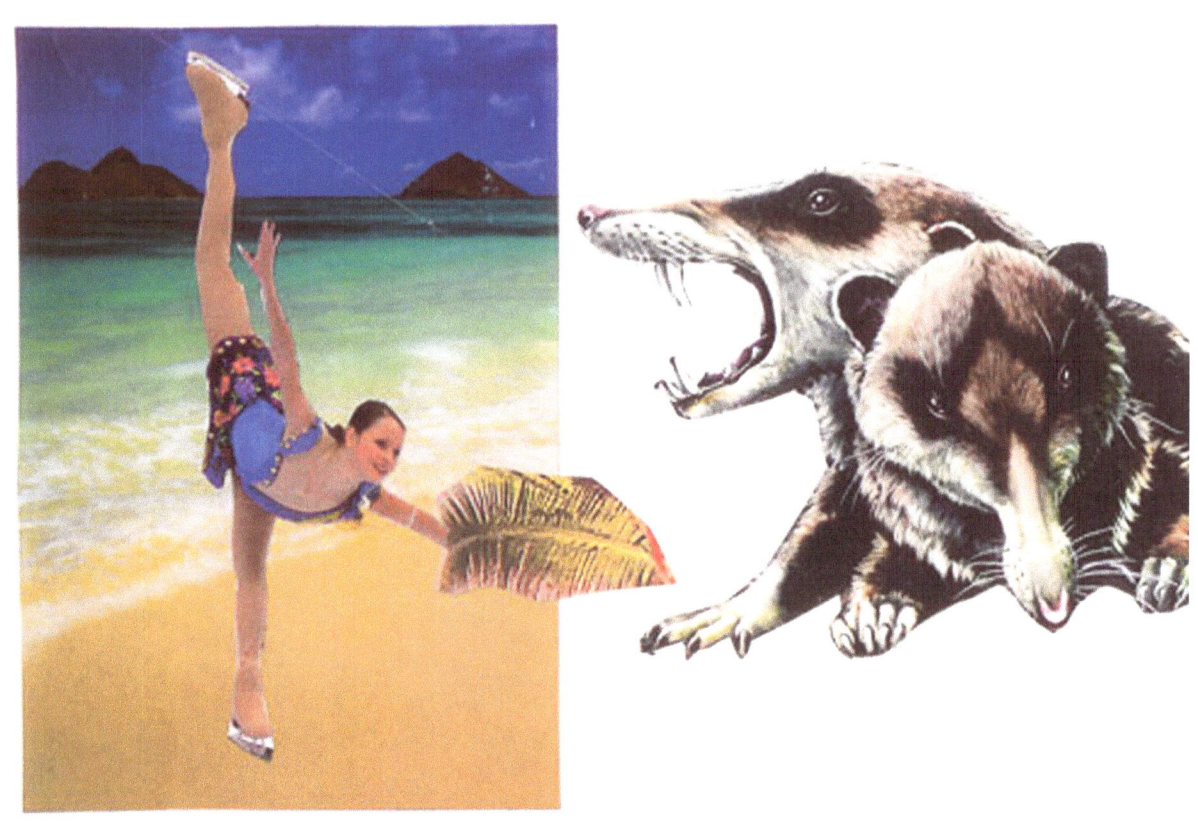

Postcard 1, 4x6"

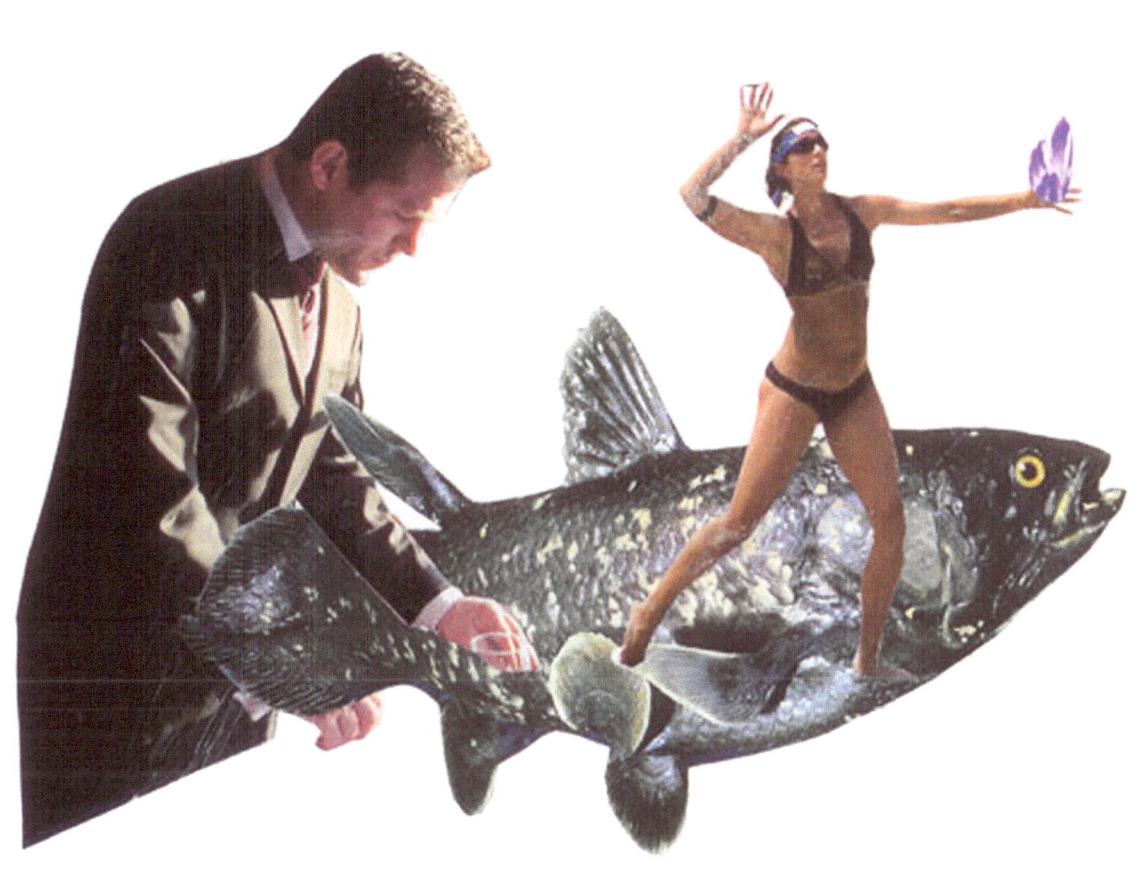

Postcard 2, 4x6"

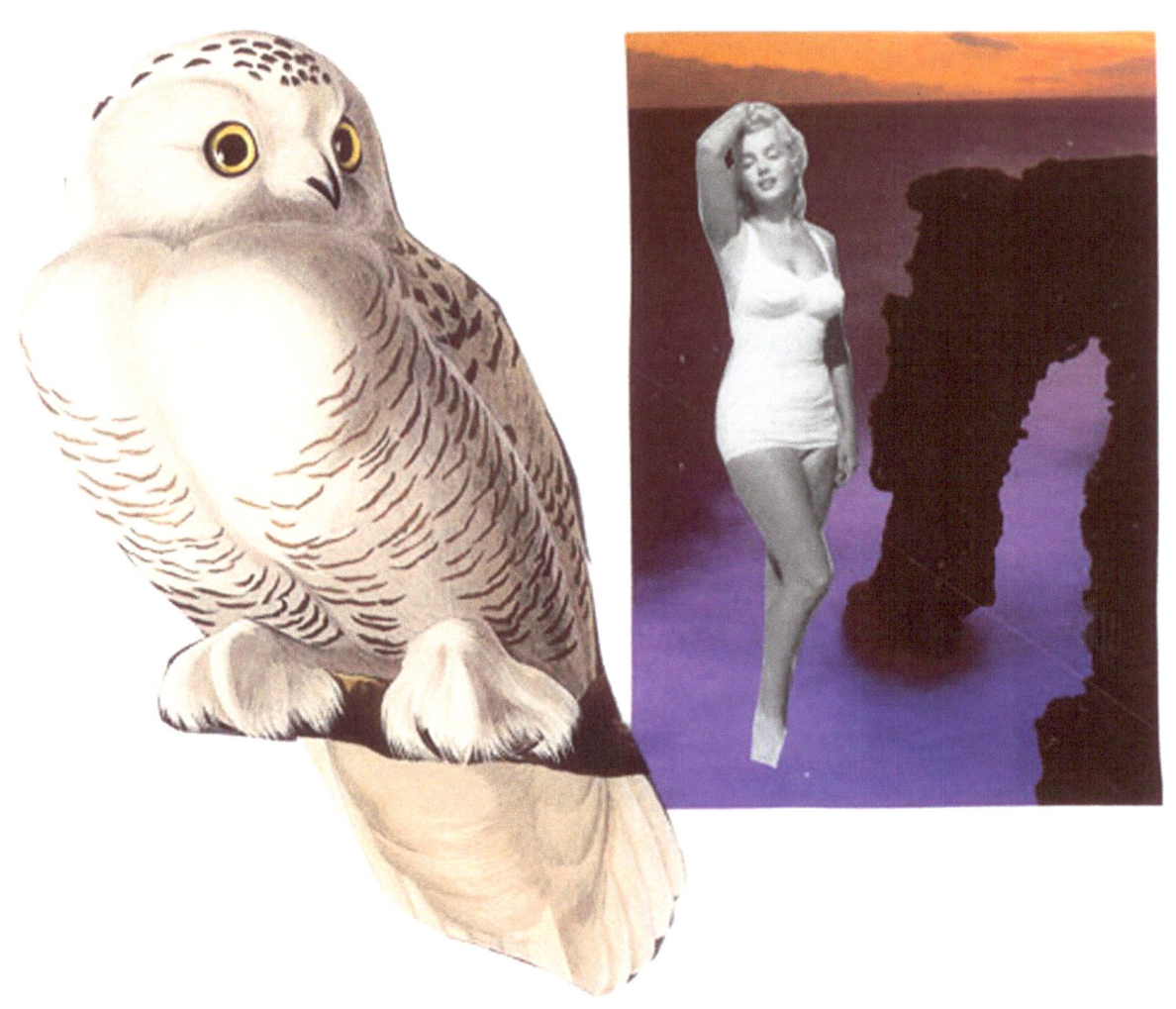

Postcard 3, 4x6"

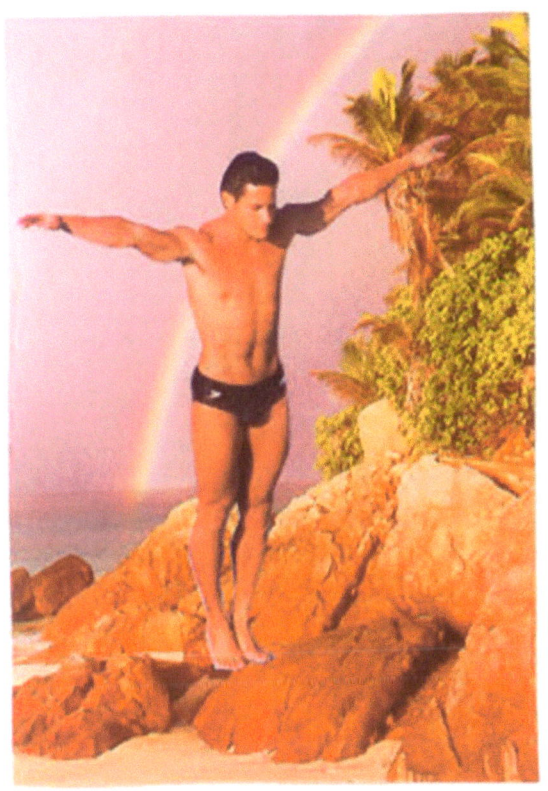
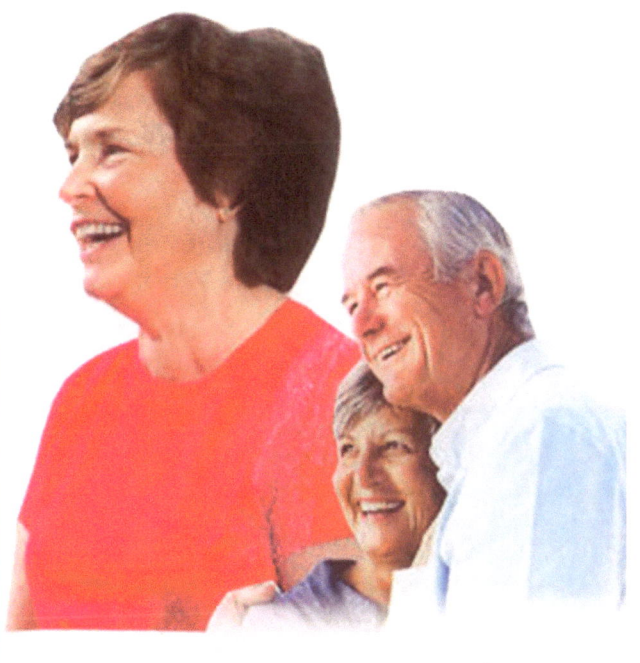

Postcard 4, 4x6"

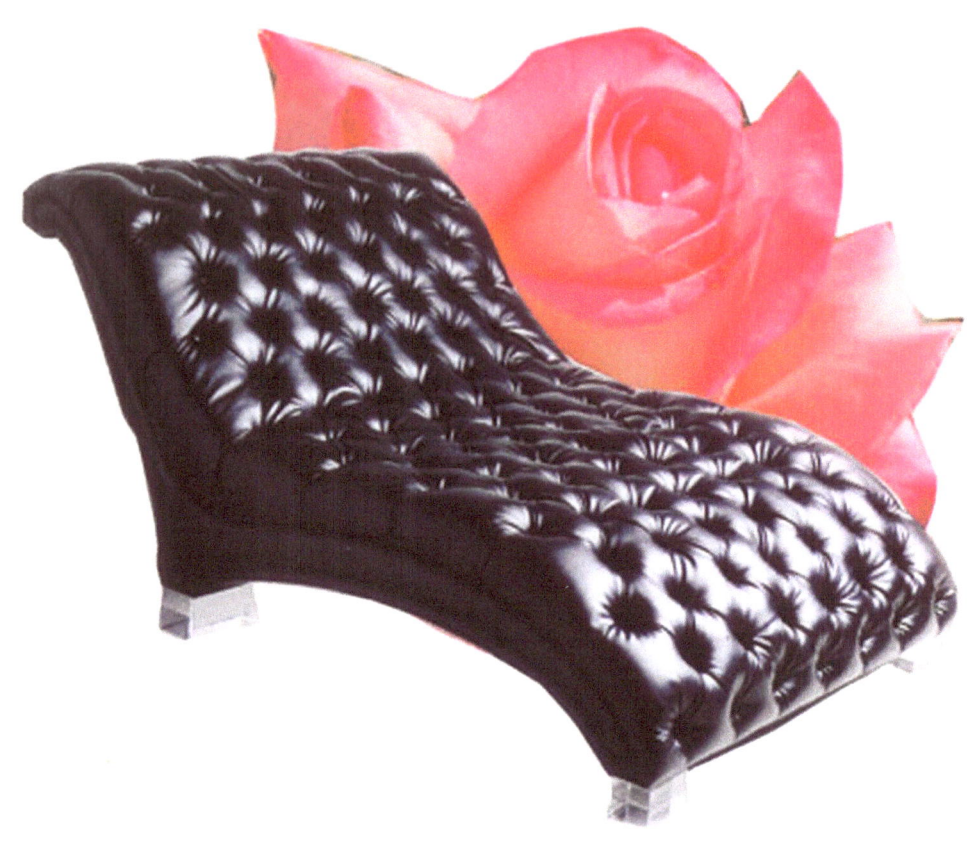

Postcard 5, 4x6"

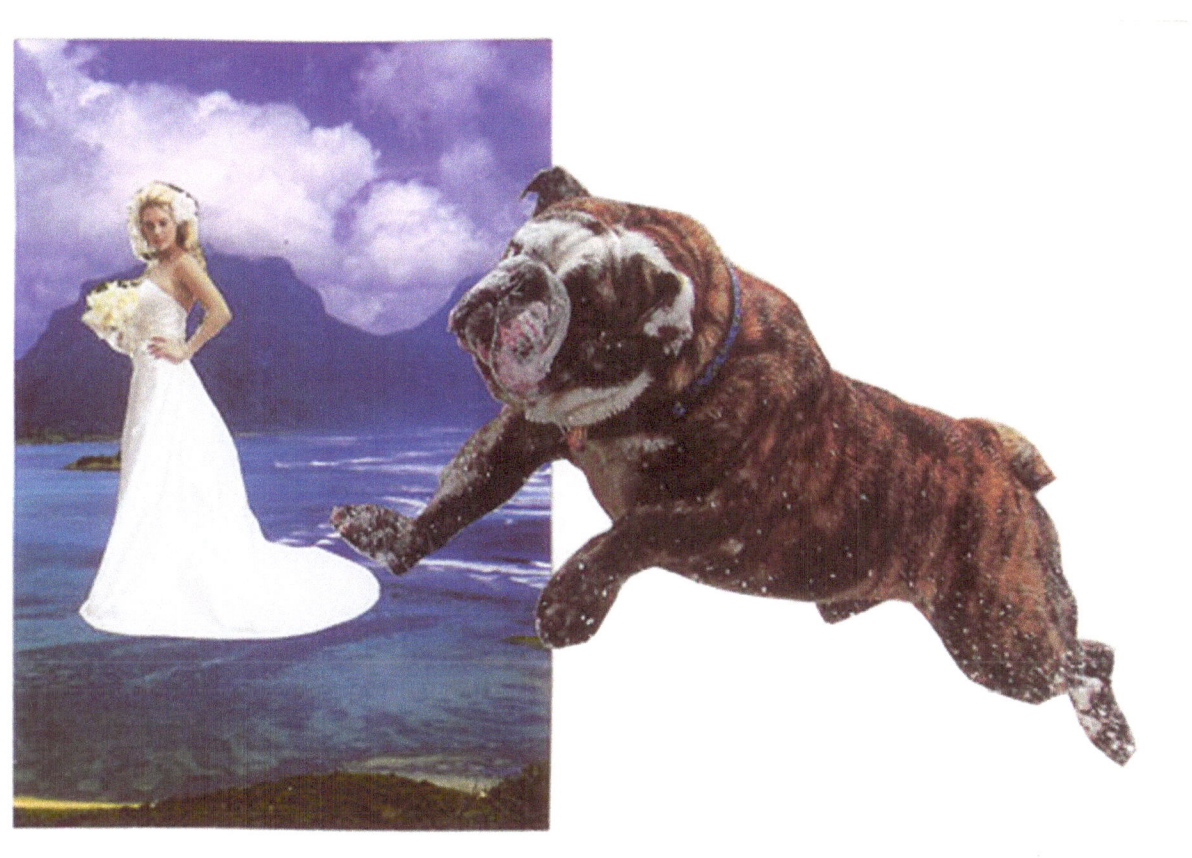

Postcard 6, 4x6"

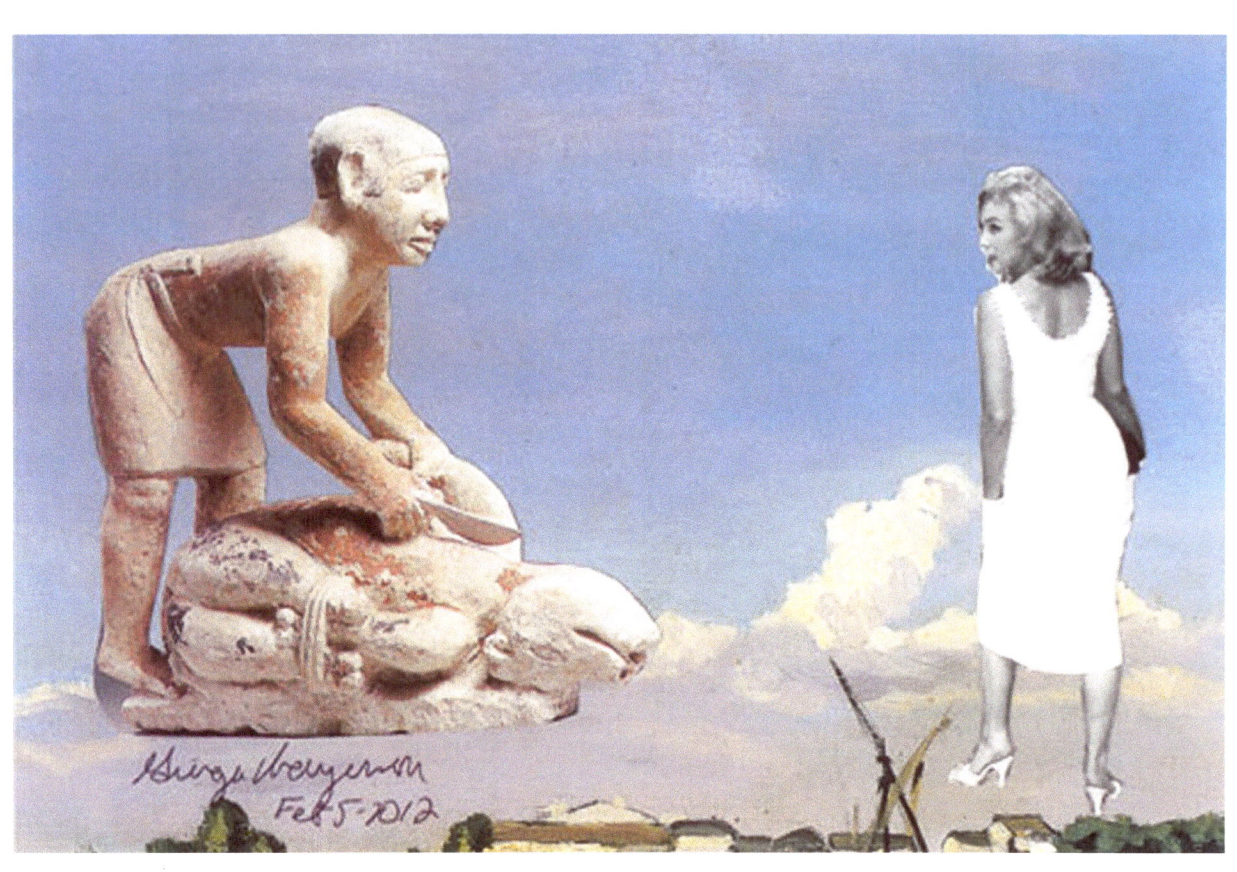

Postcard 7, 4x6"

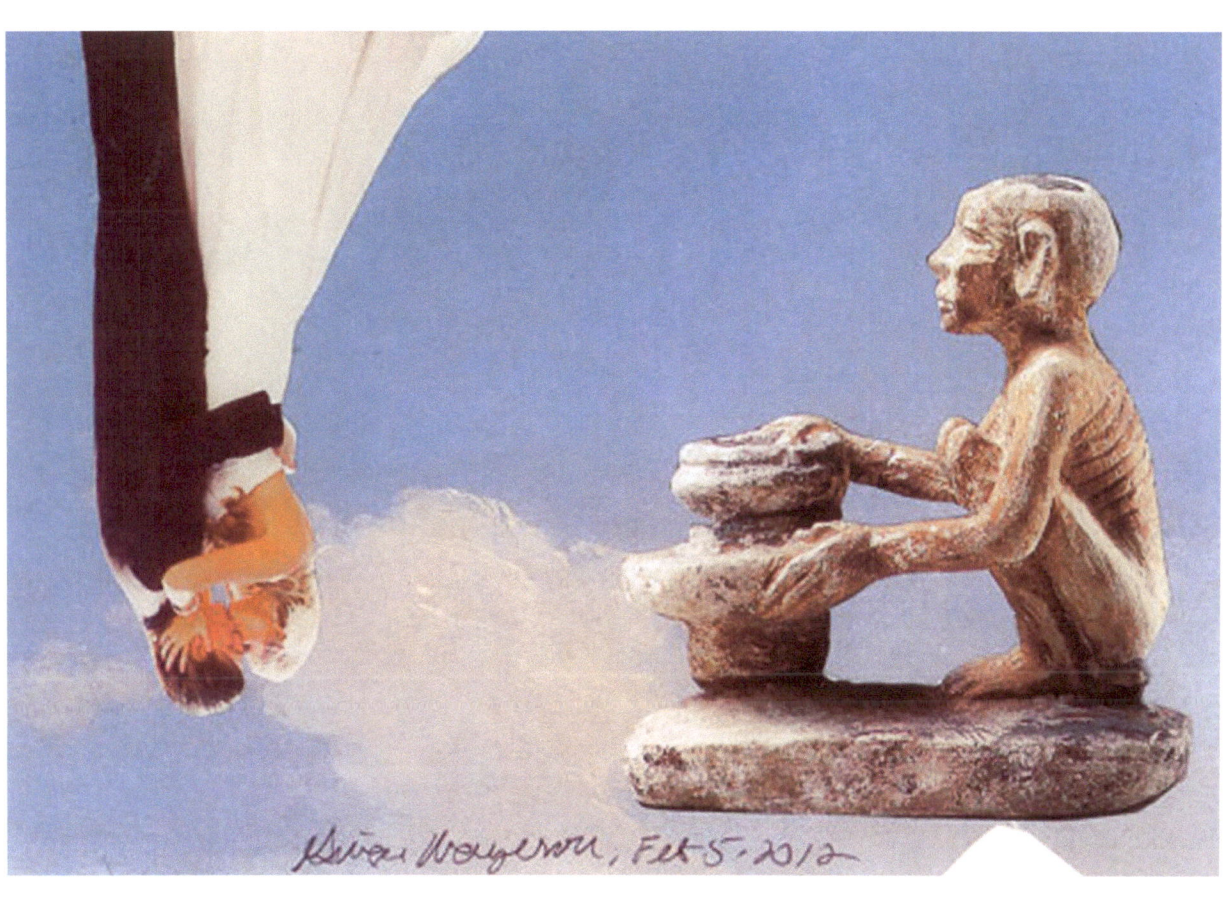

Postcard 8, 4x6"

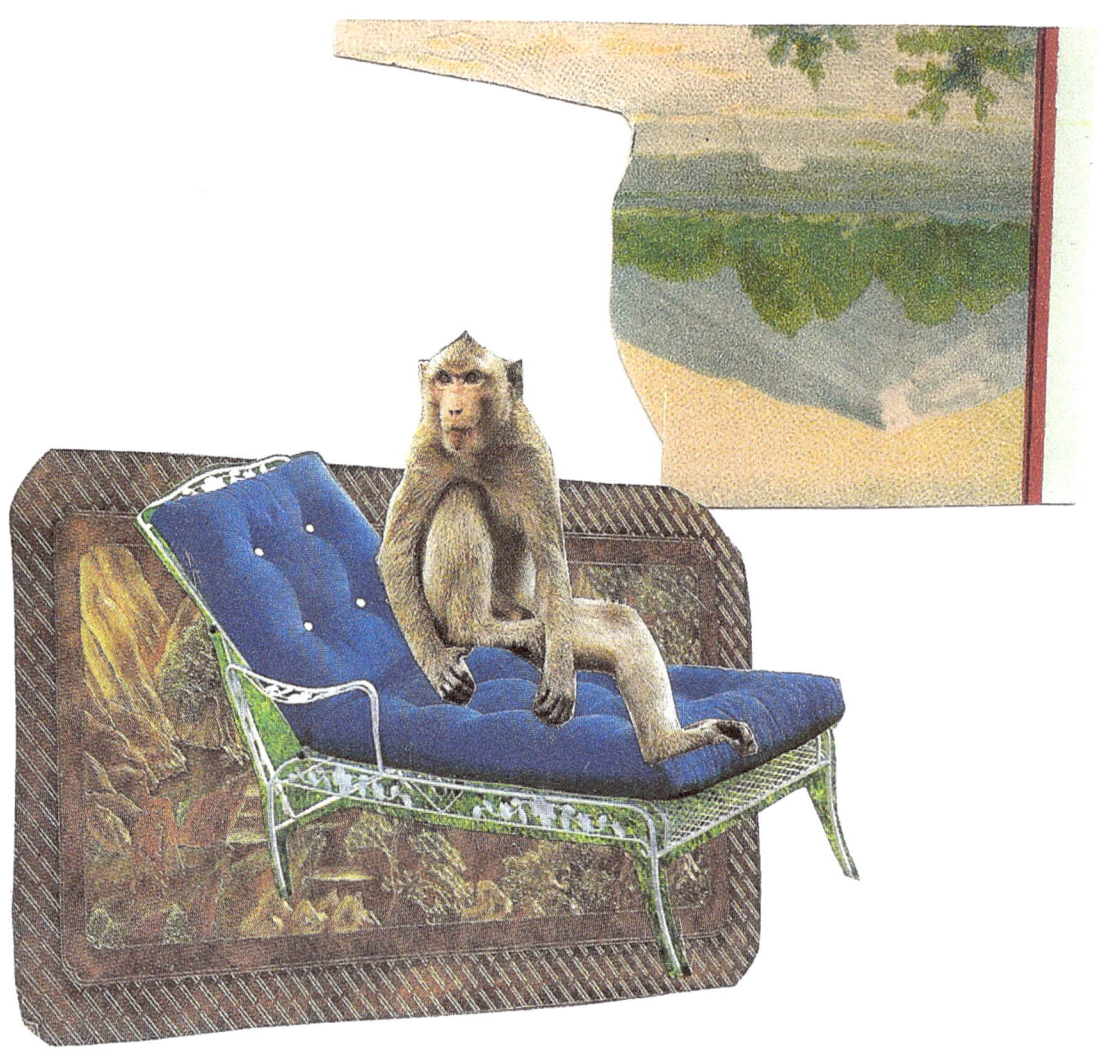

Primate Chaise, 5.5x5.5"

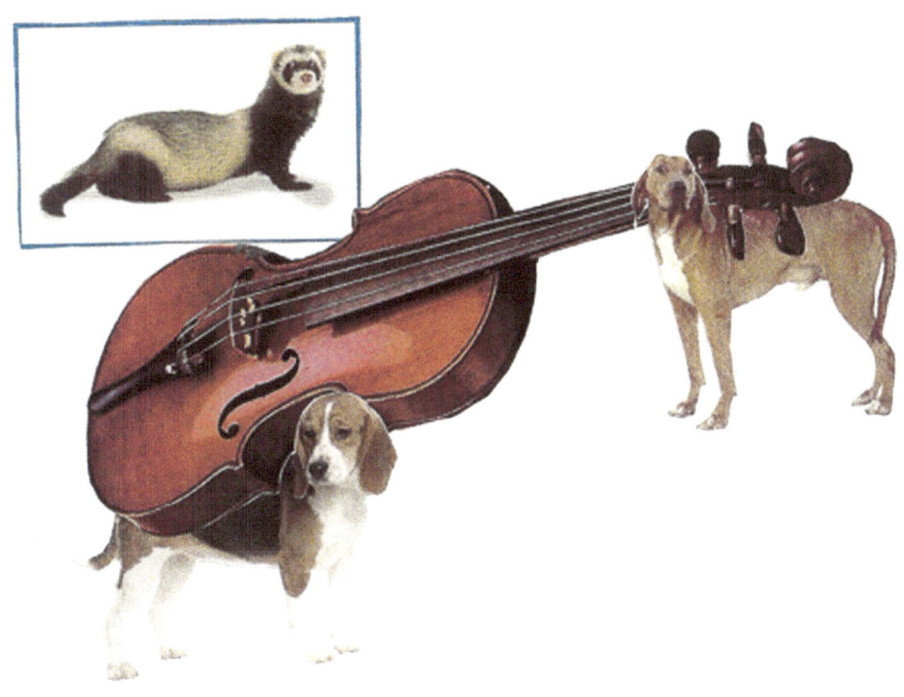

Quartet, 4x6"

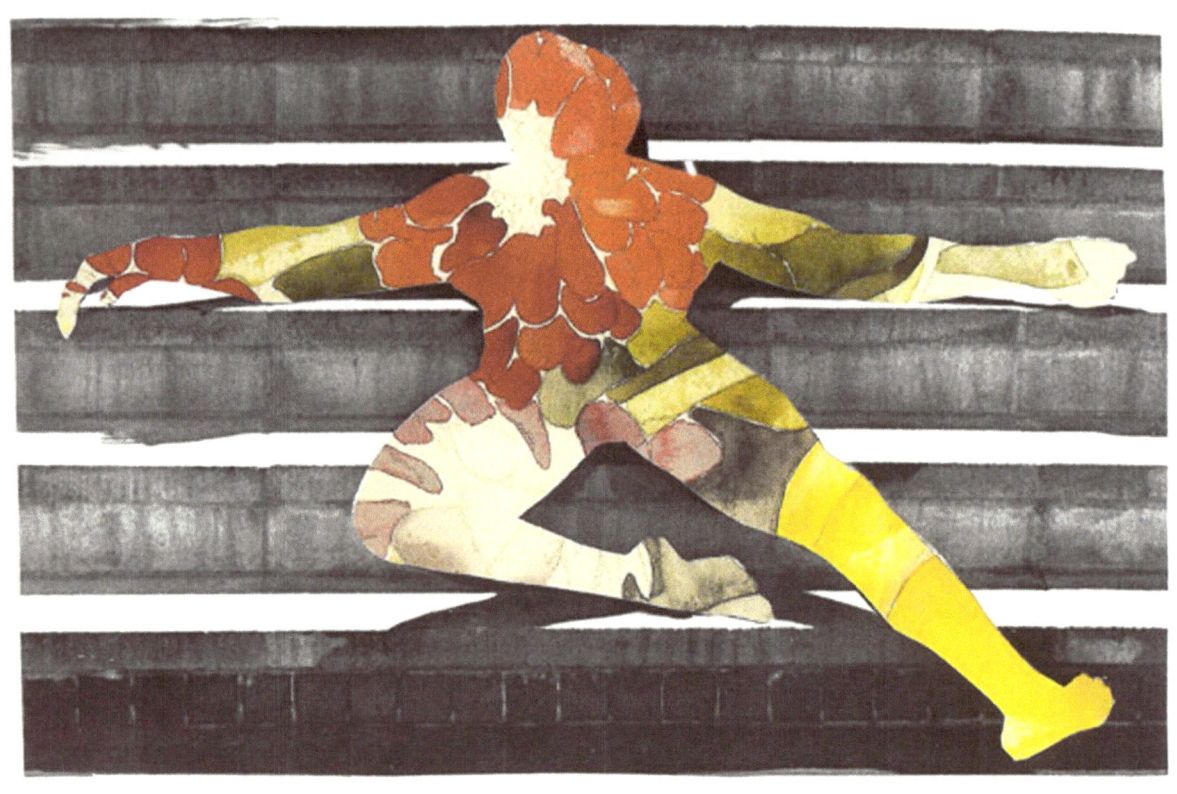

Shadows, 5.5x8"

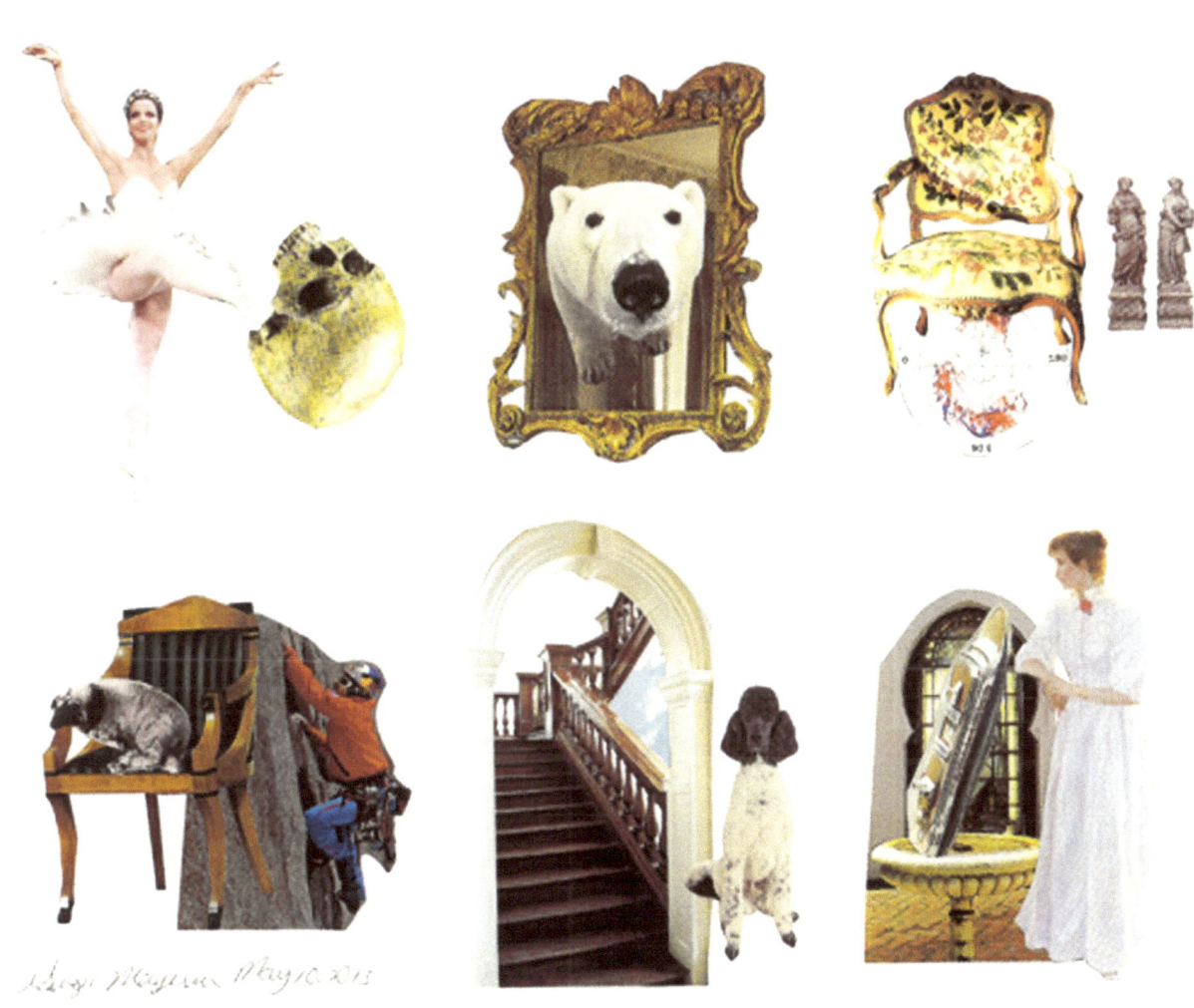

Sextet, 9x12"

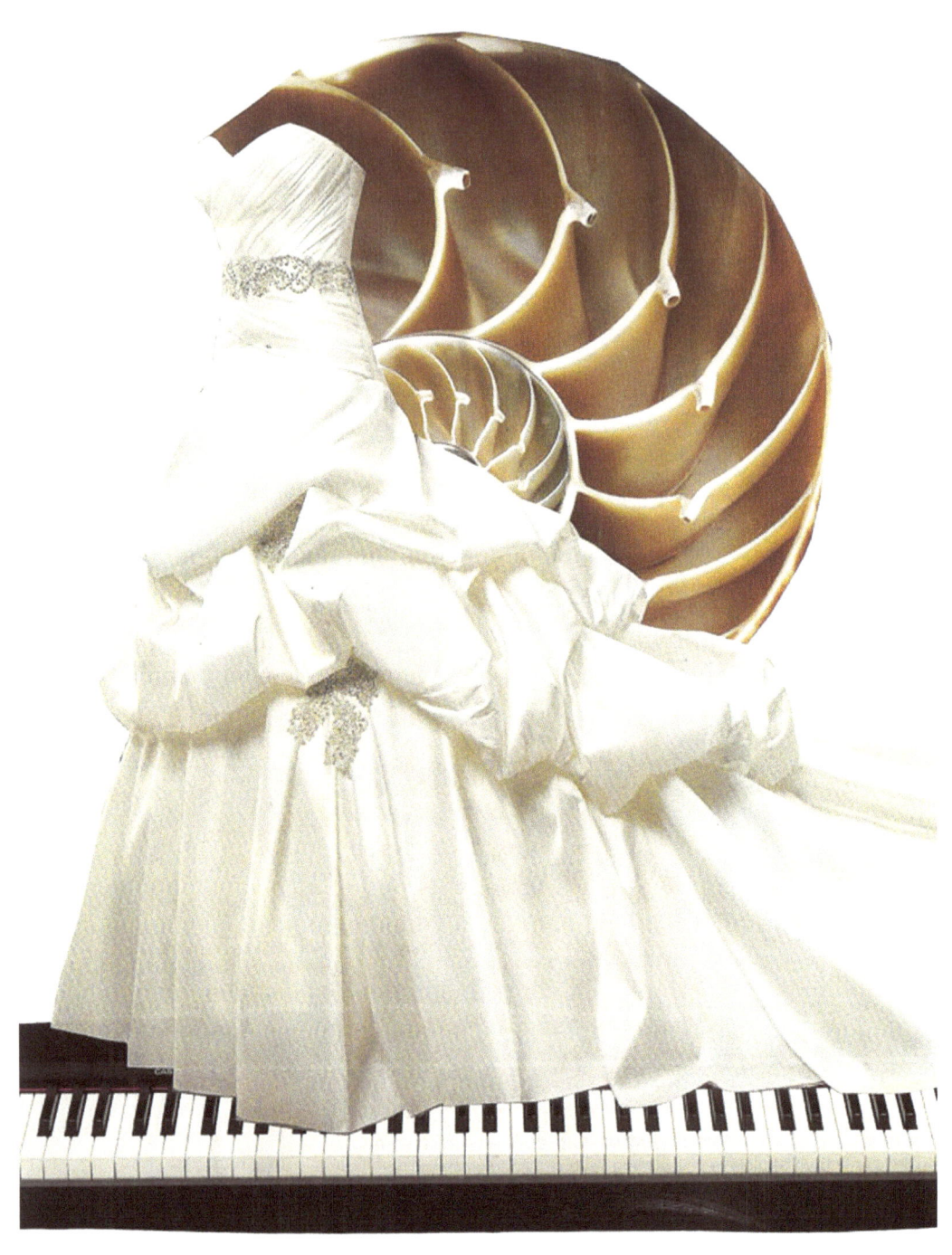

Shell Dress, 10x7"

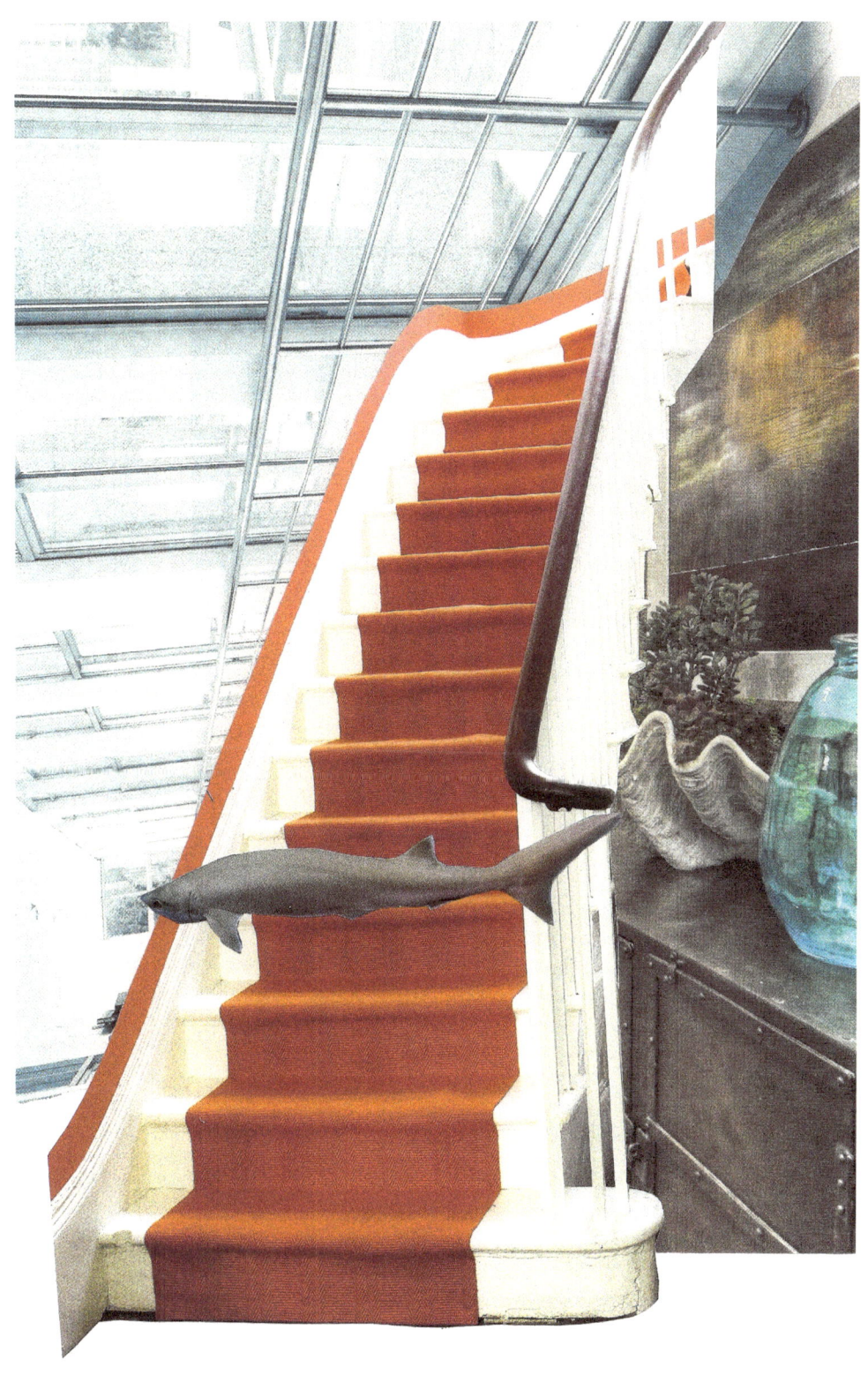

Sharkcase, 10x7"

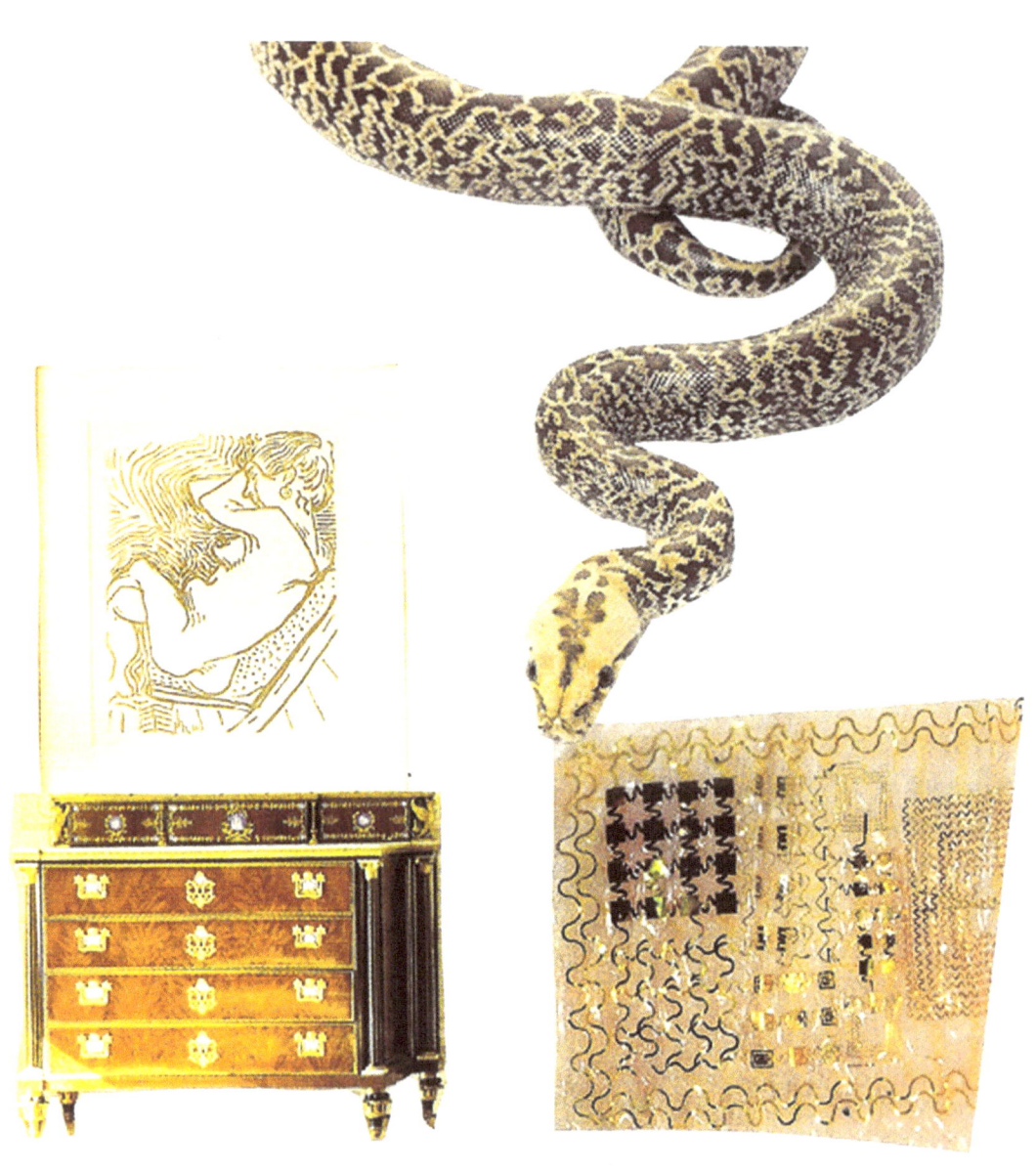

Snake Chest, 5.5x5.5"

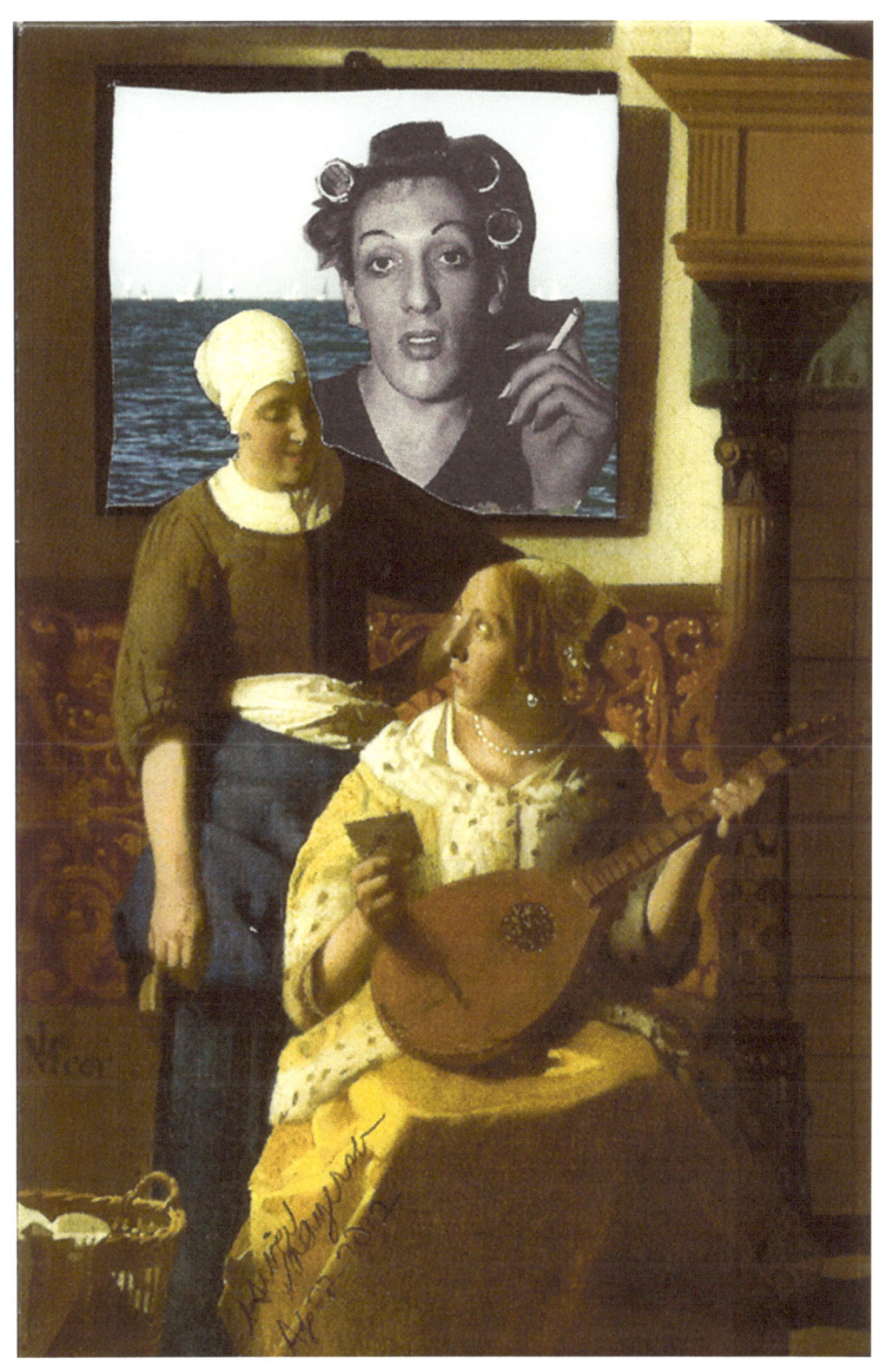

So, girls..., 6x4"

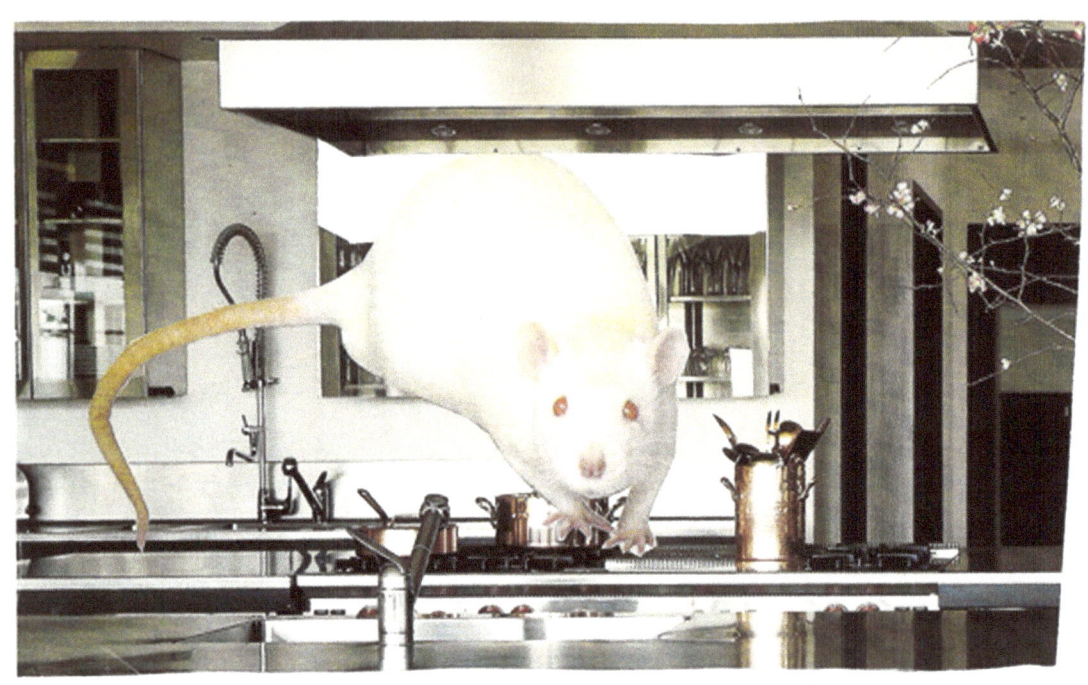

Stainless Rat, 5.5x8"

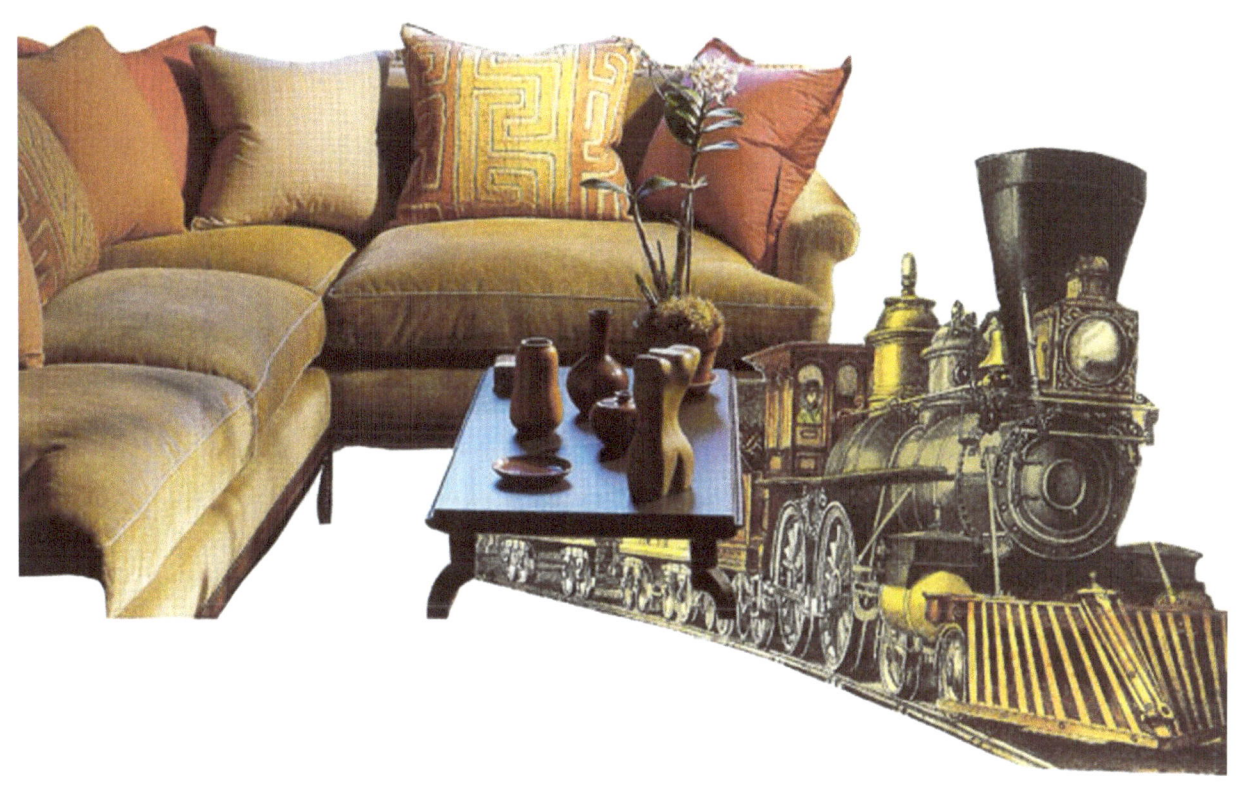

Sofa Train, 10x7"

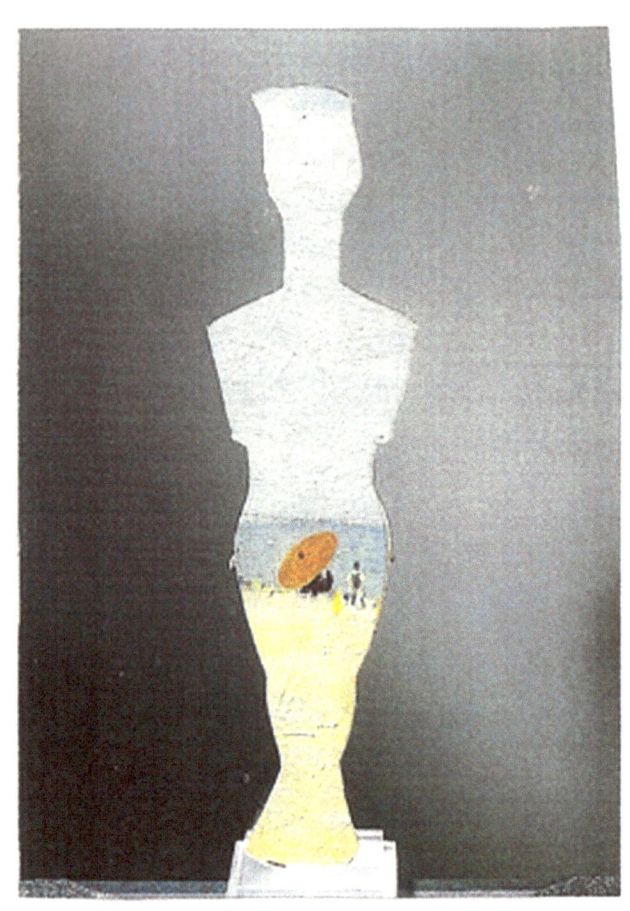

Statue, 5.5x5.5"

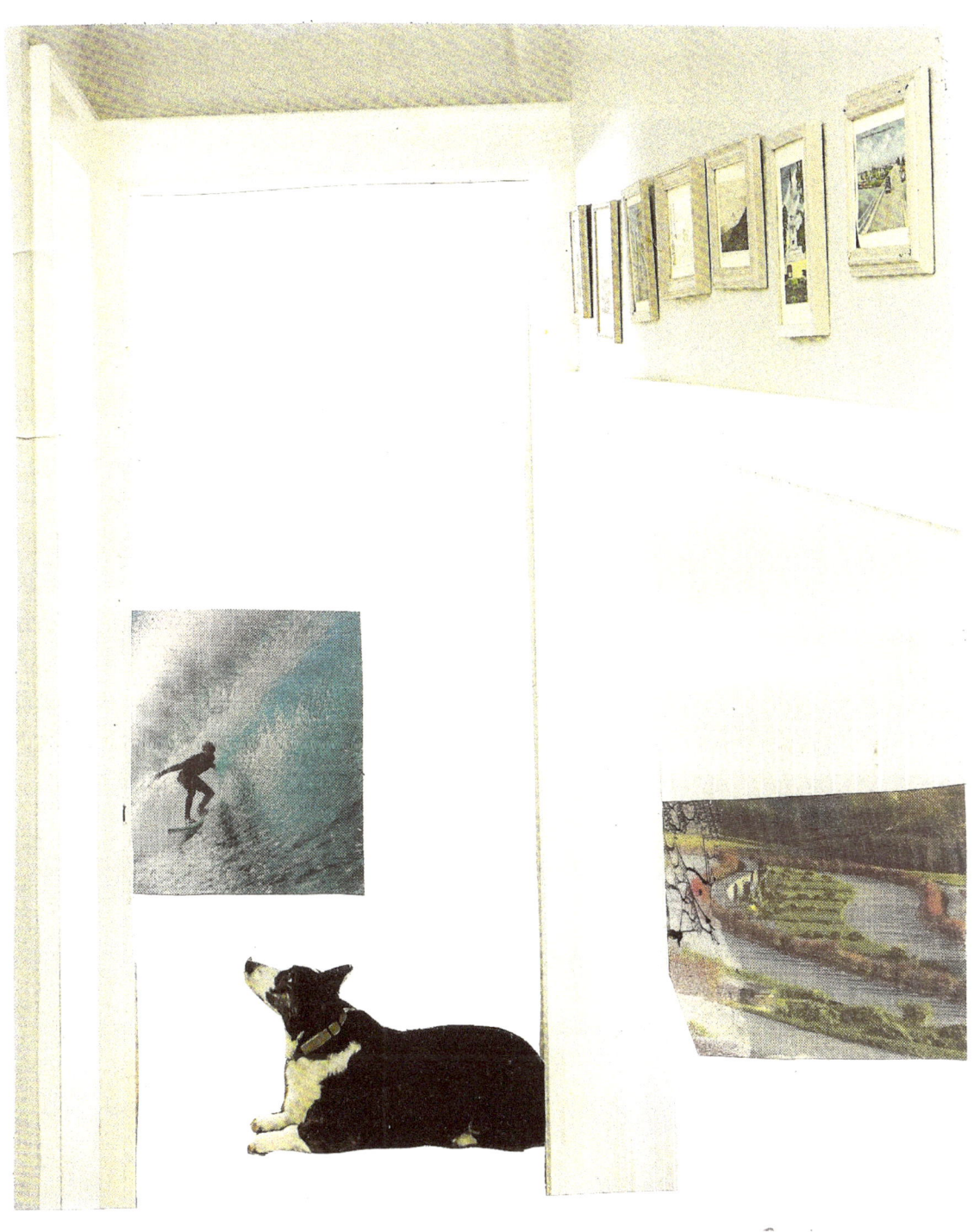

Surfer Pup, 8x5.5"

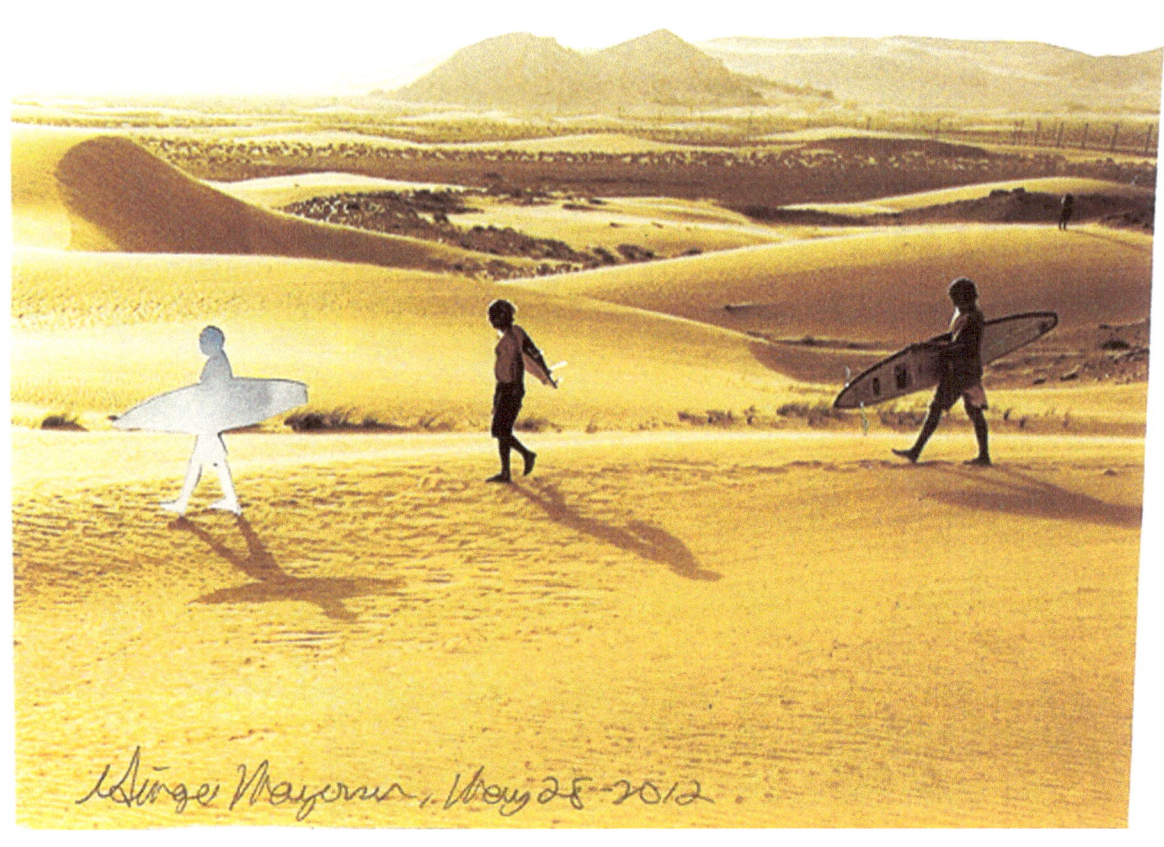

Surfers, 4x6"

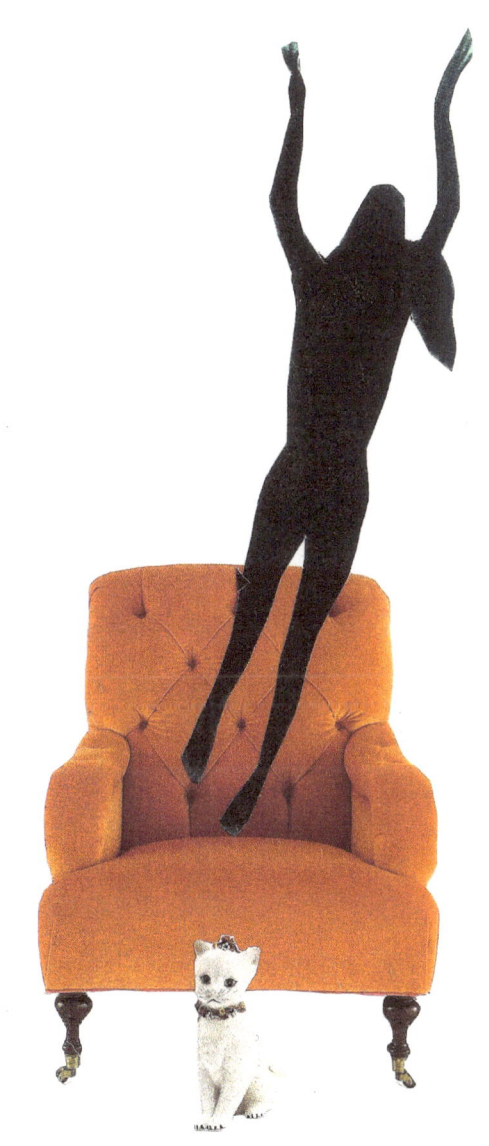

Swimmer, 8x5.5"

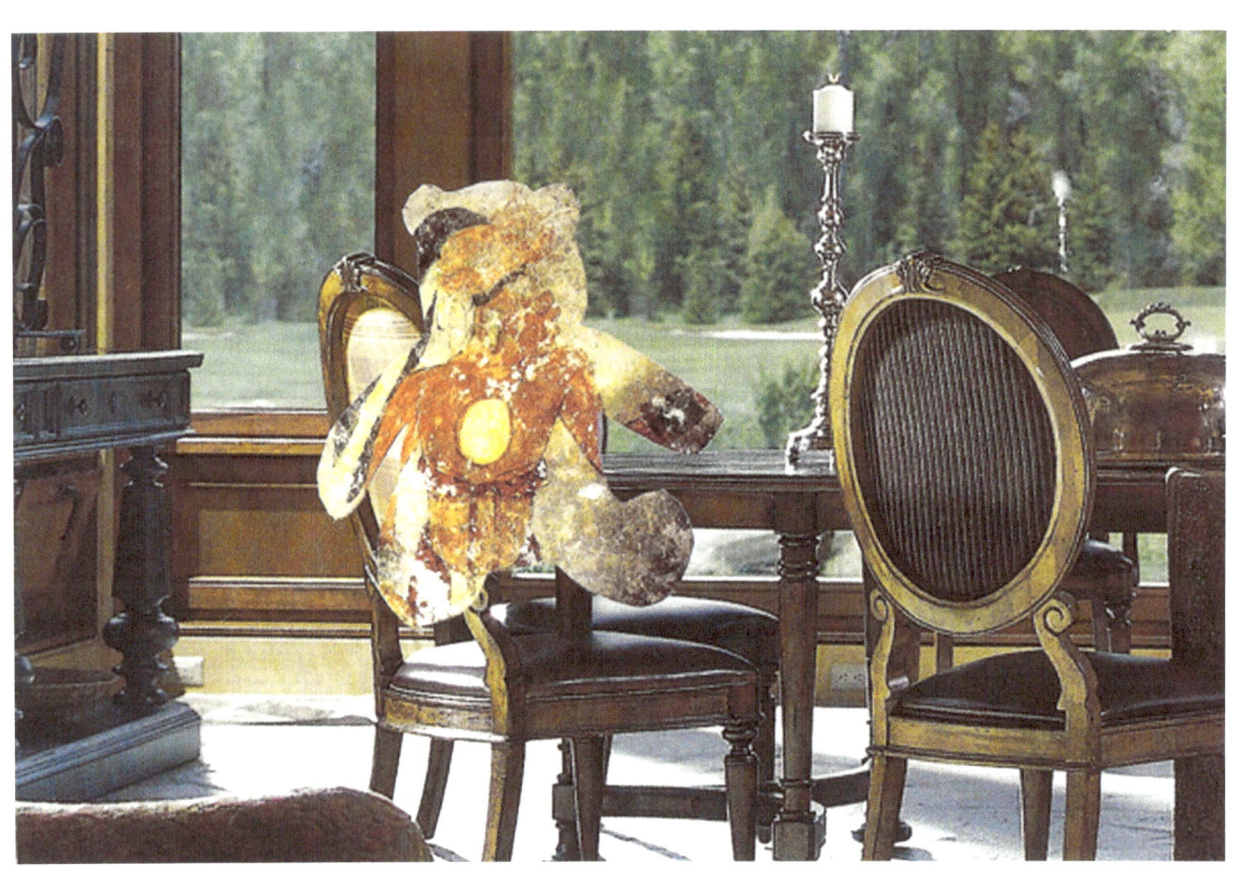

Teddy Bear Lost, 4x6"

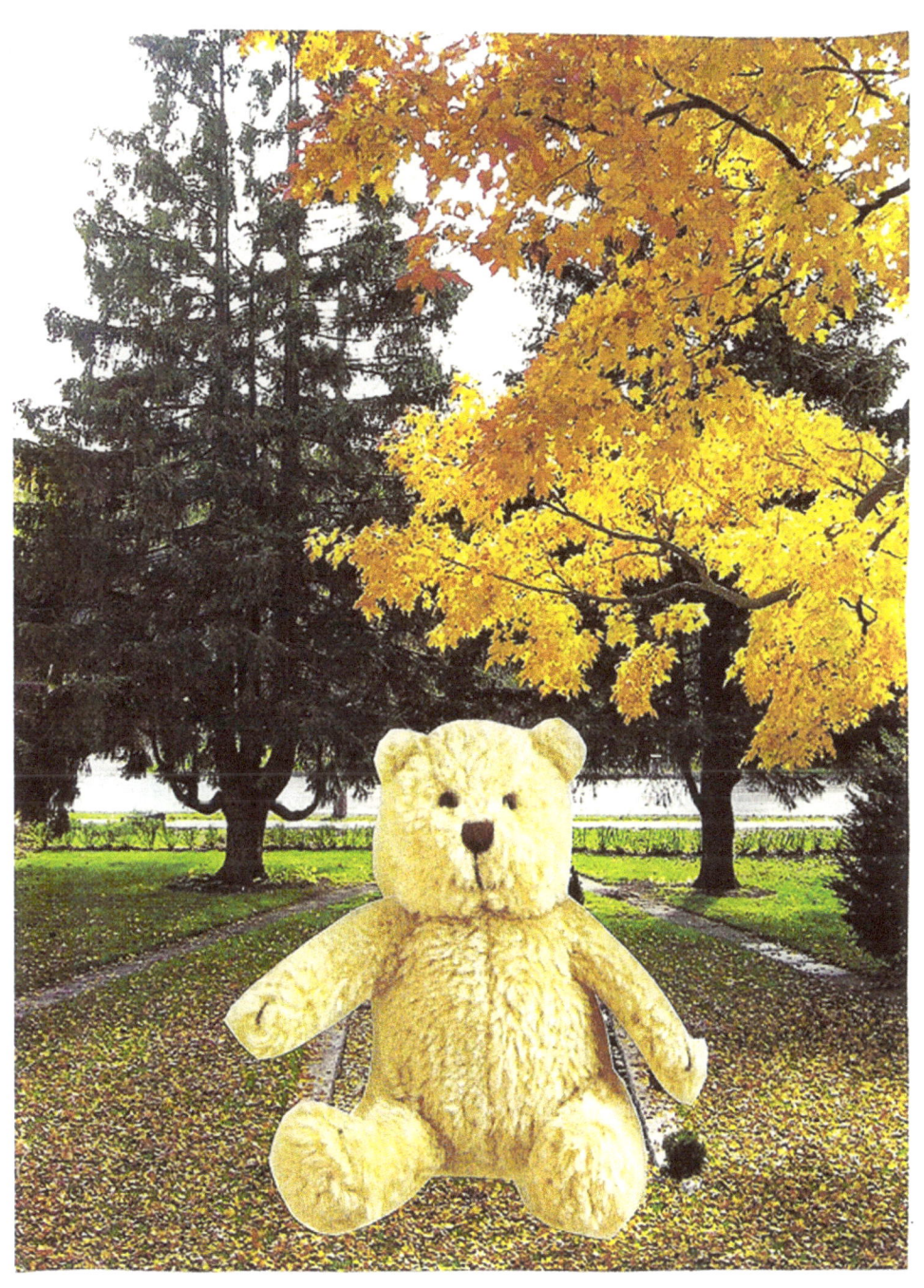

Teddy Bear Found, 6x4"

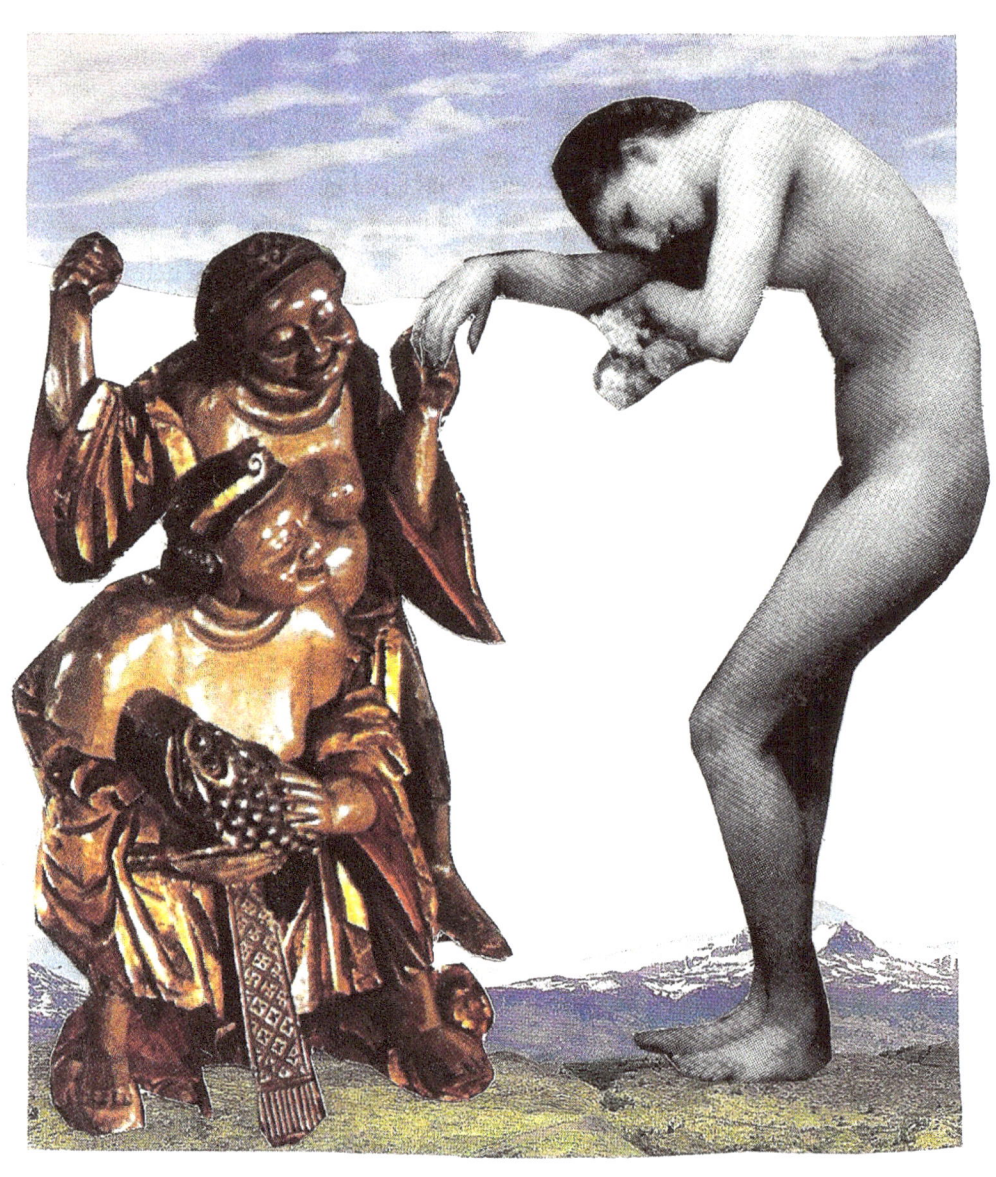

The Engagement, 5.5x5.5"

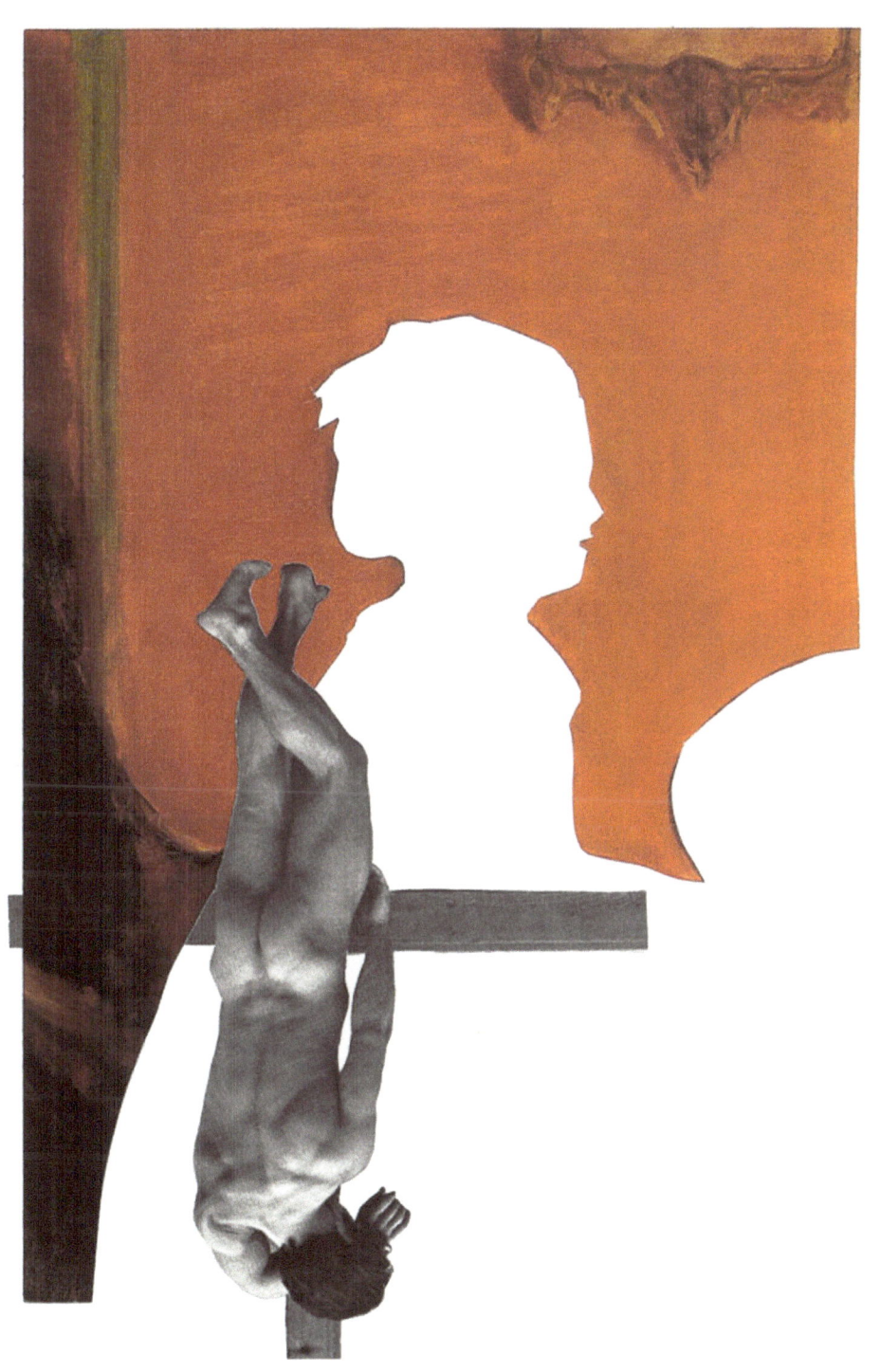

The Hanged Man, 10x7"

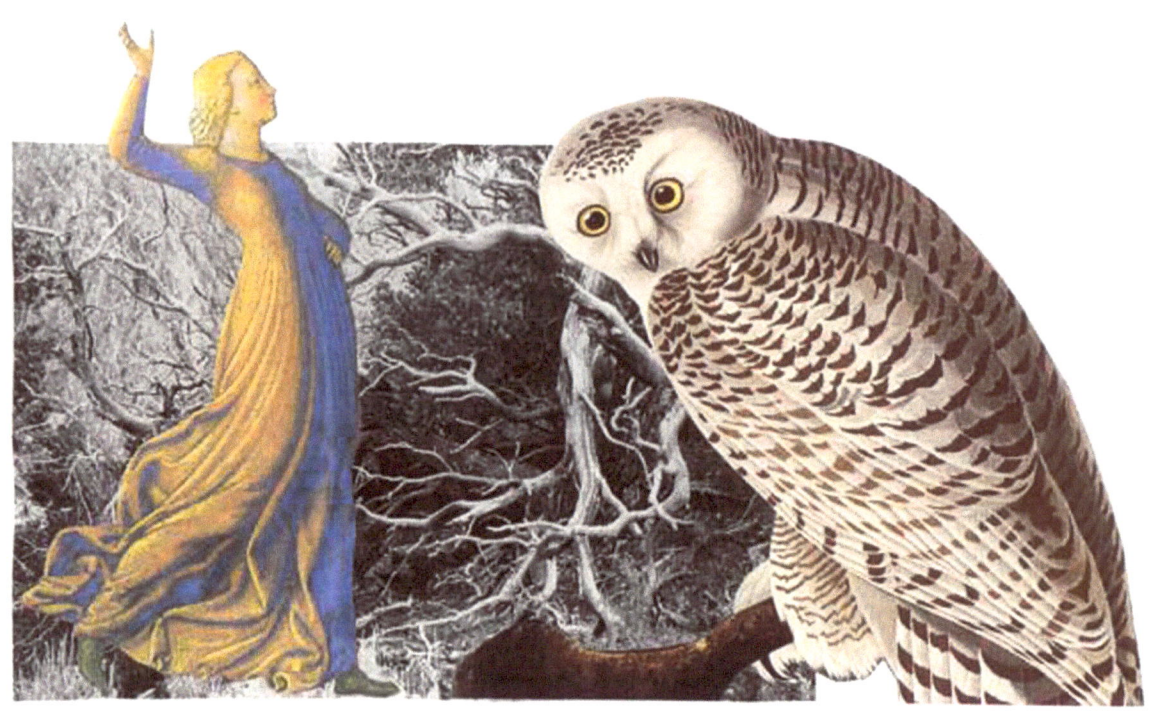

The Late Show, 5.5x8"

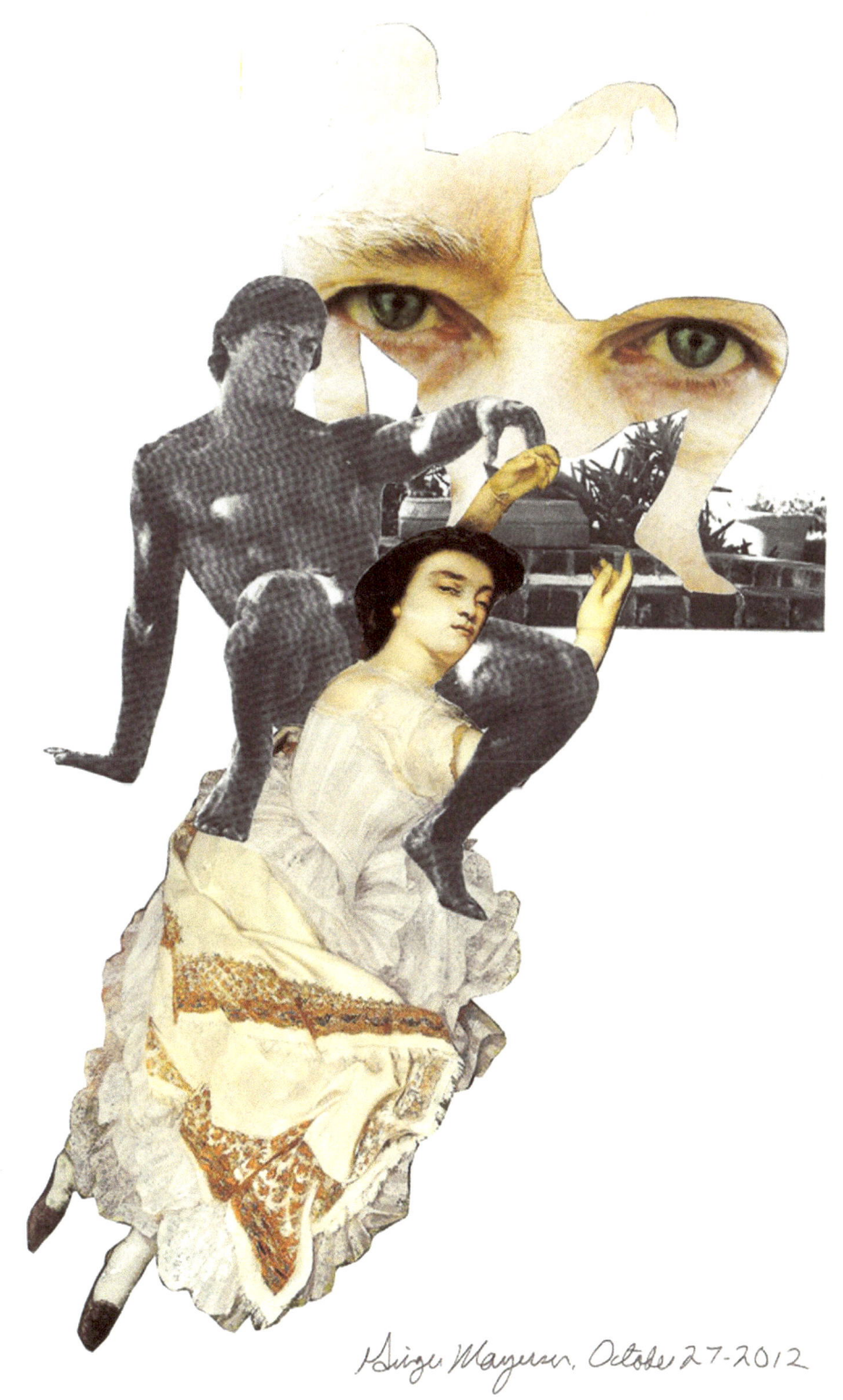

The Lovers and Guest, 10x7"

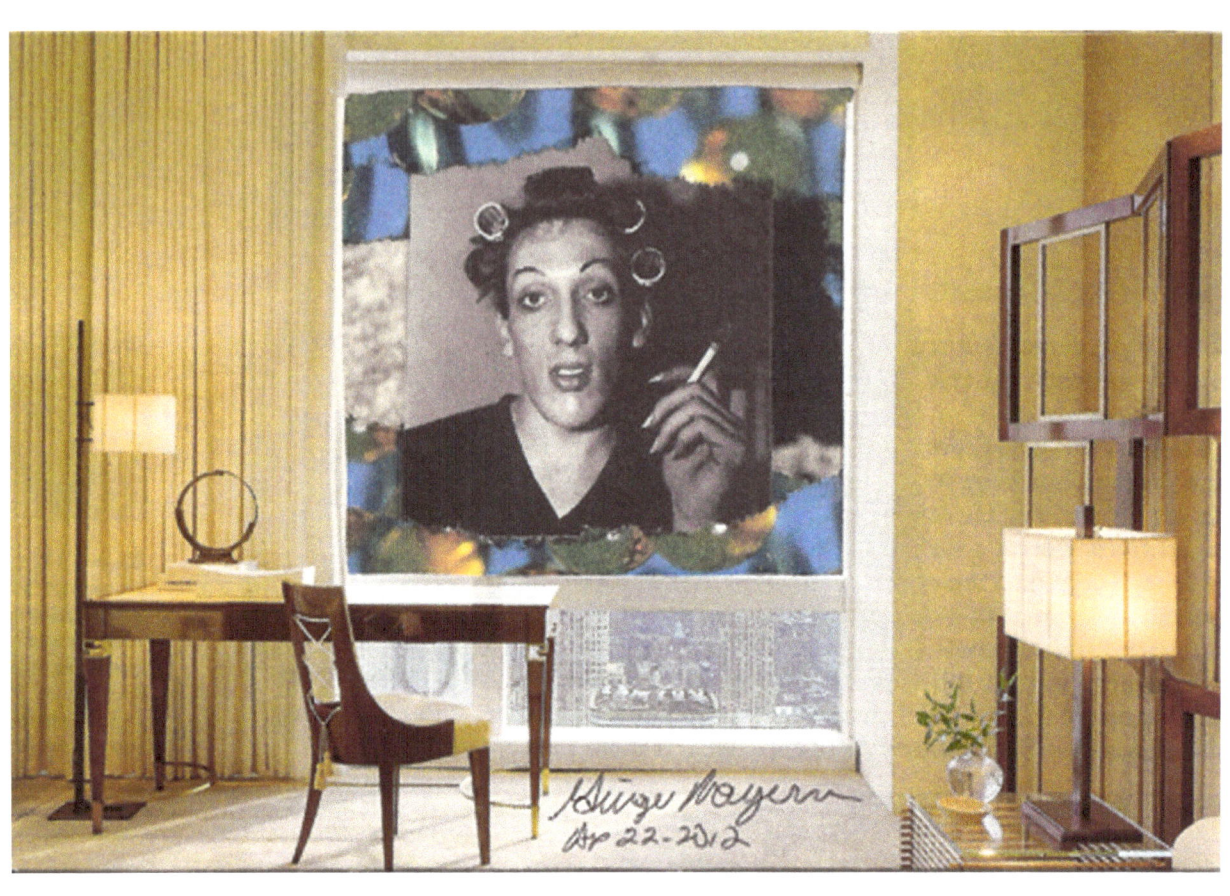

Then I was saying to Diane…, 4x6"

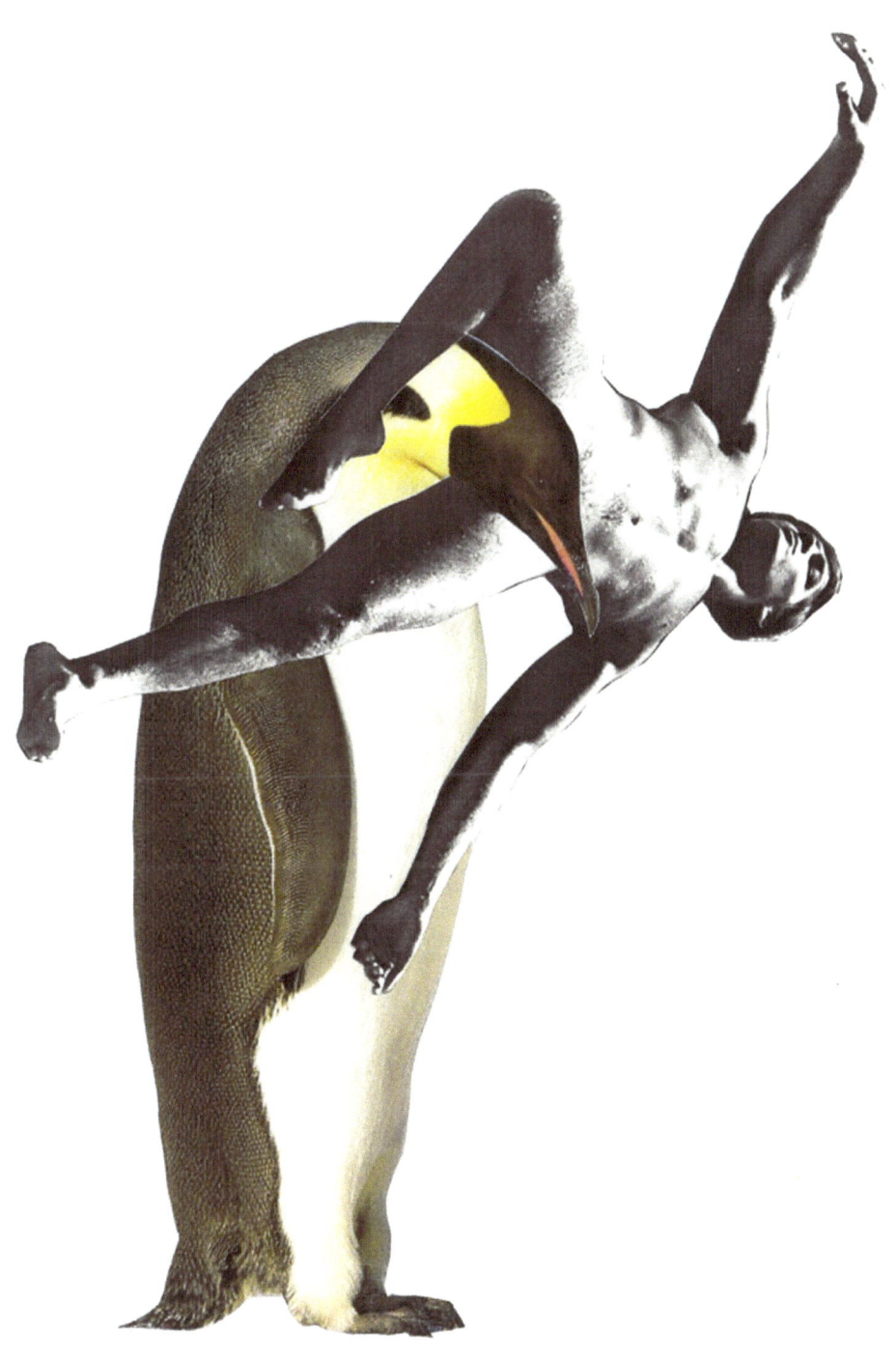

The Penguinist, 10x7"

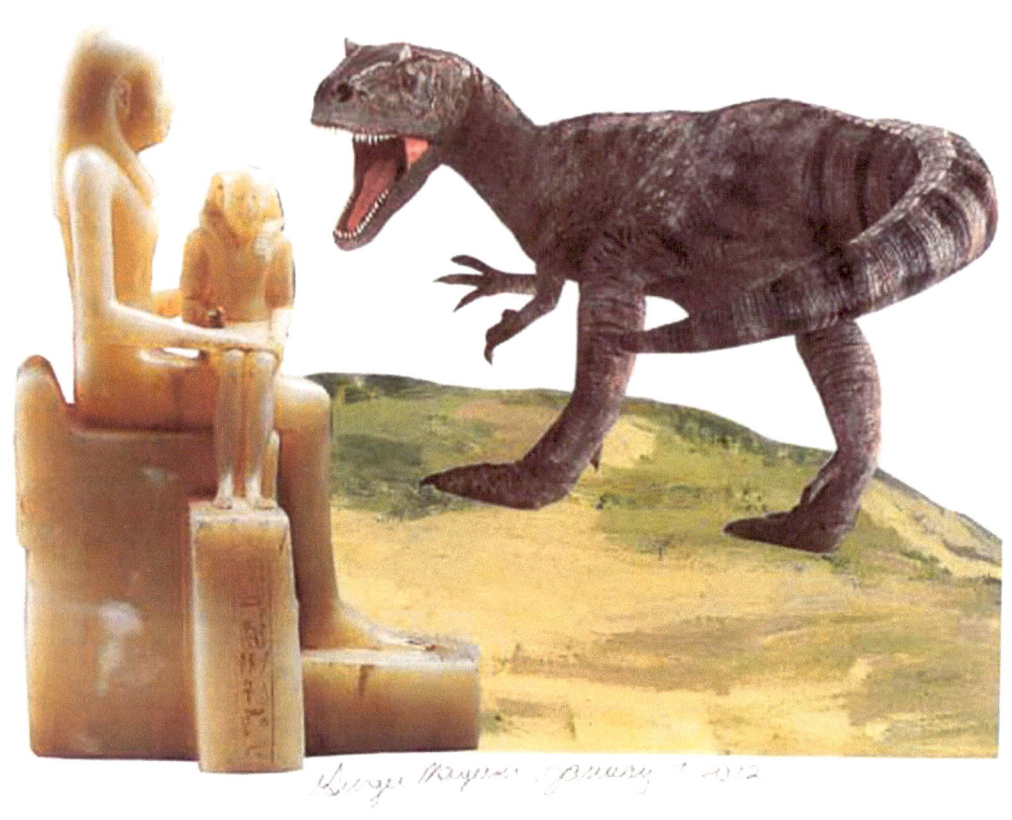

Threat or Homage? 5.5x8″

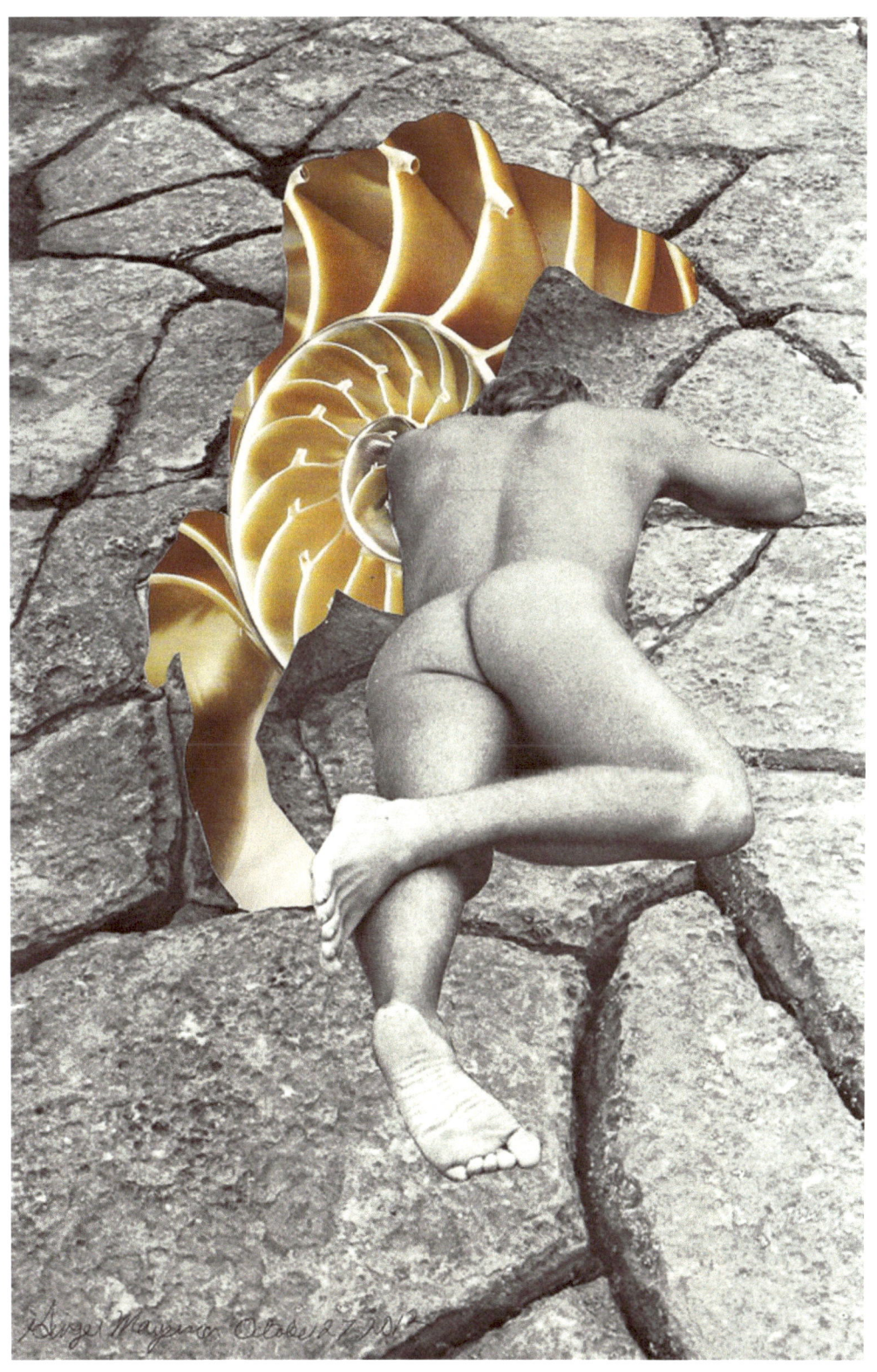

The Shell, 10x7"

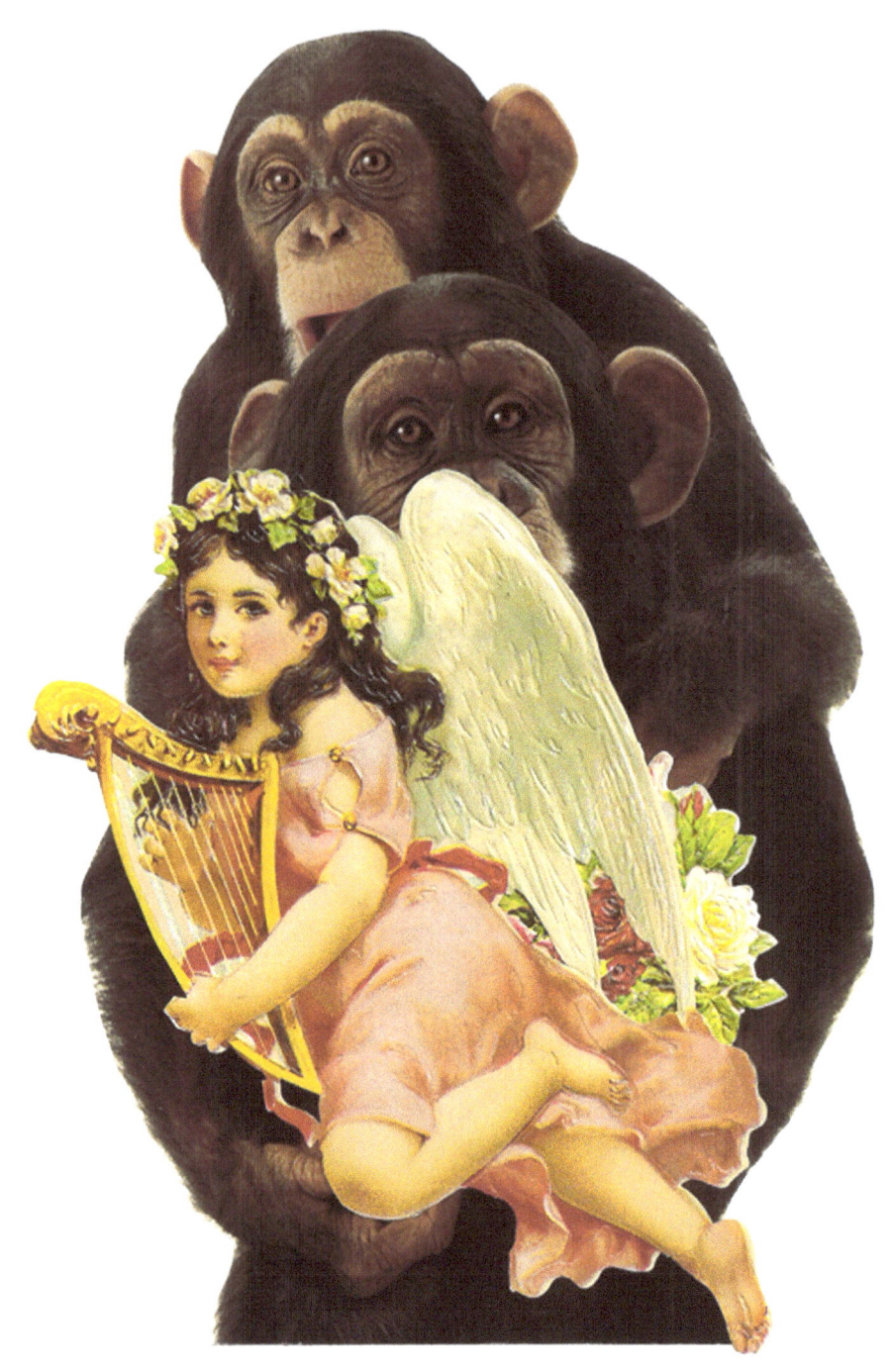

Trio, 10x7"

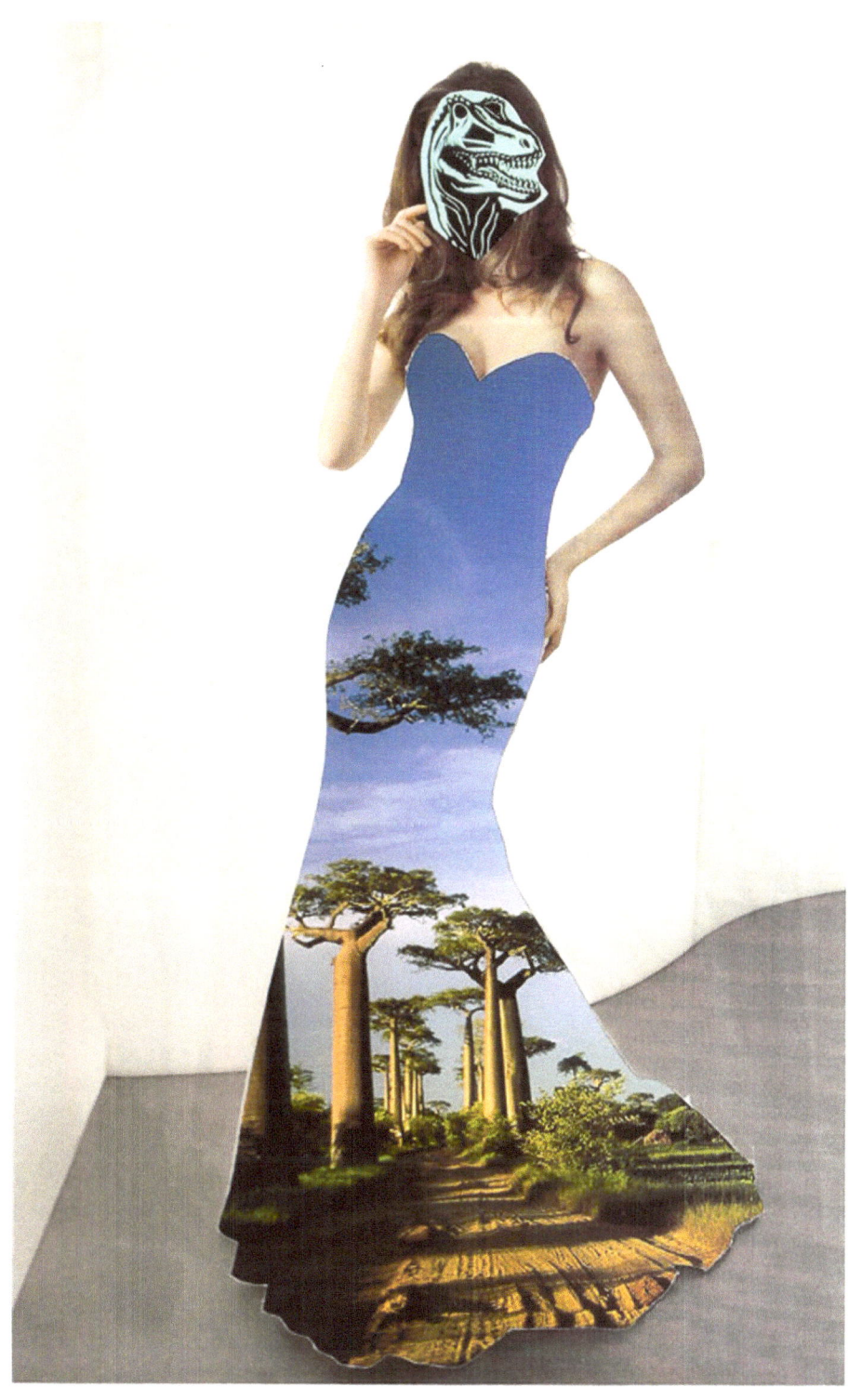

Tree Dress, 12x9"

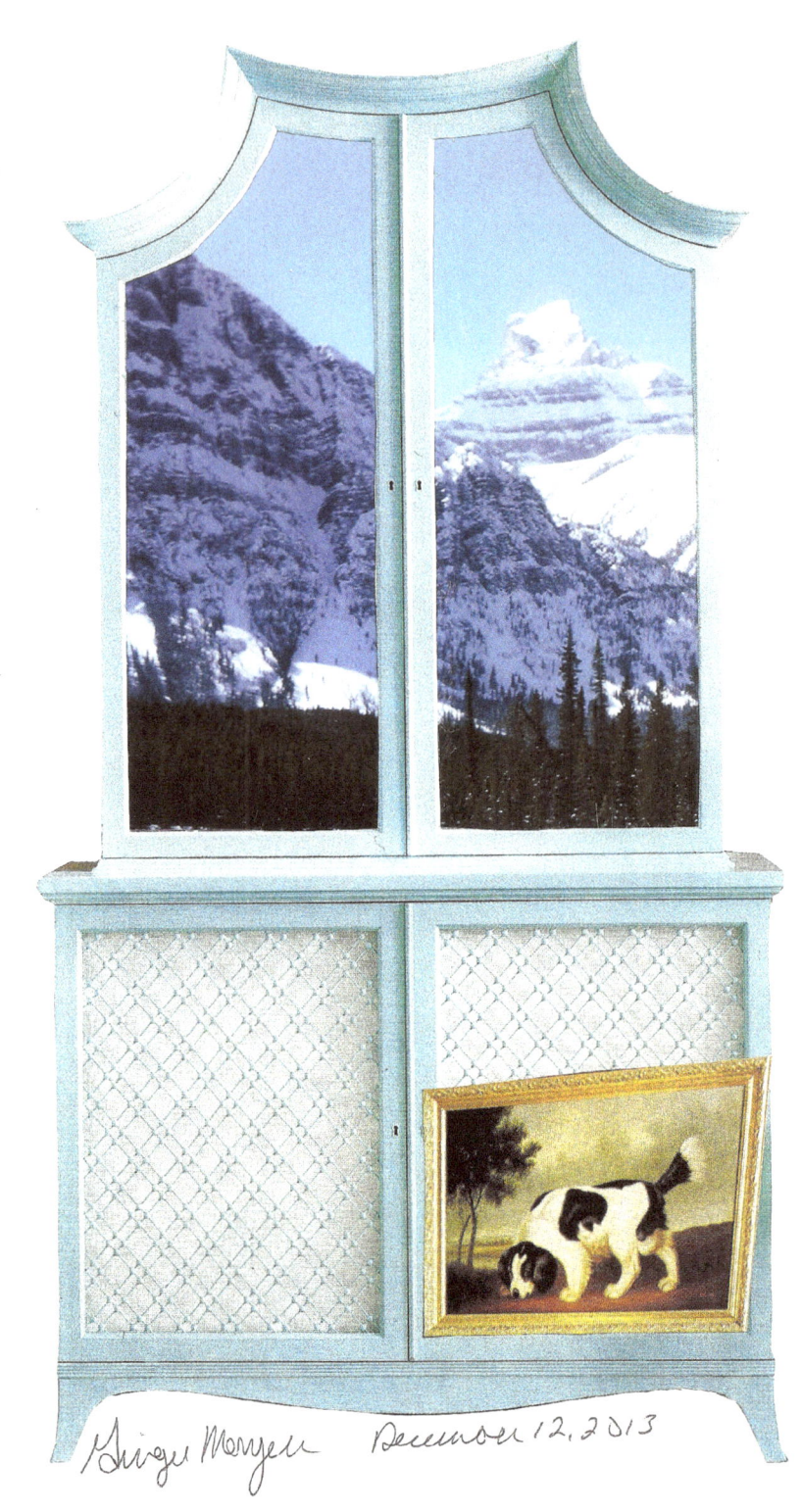

View 2, 10x7"

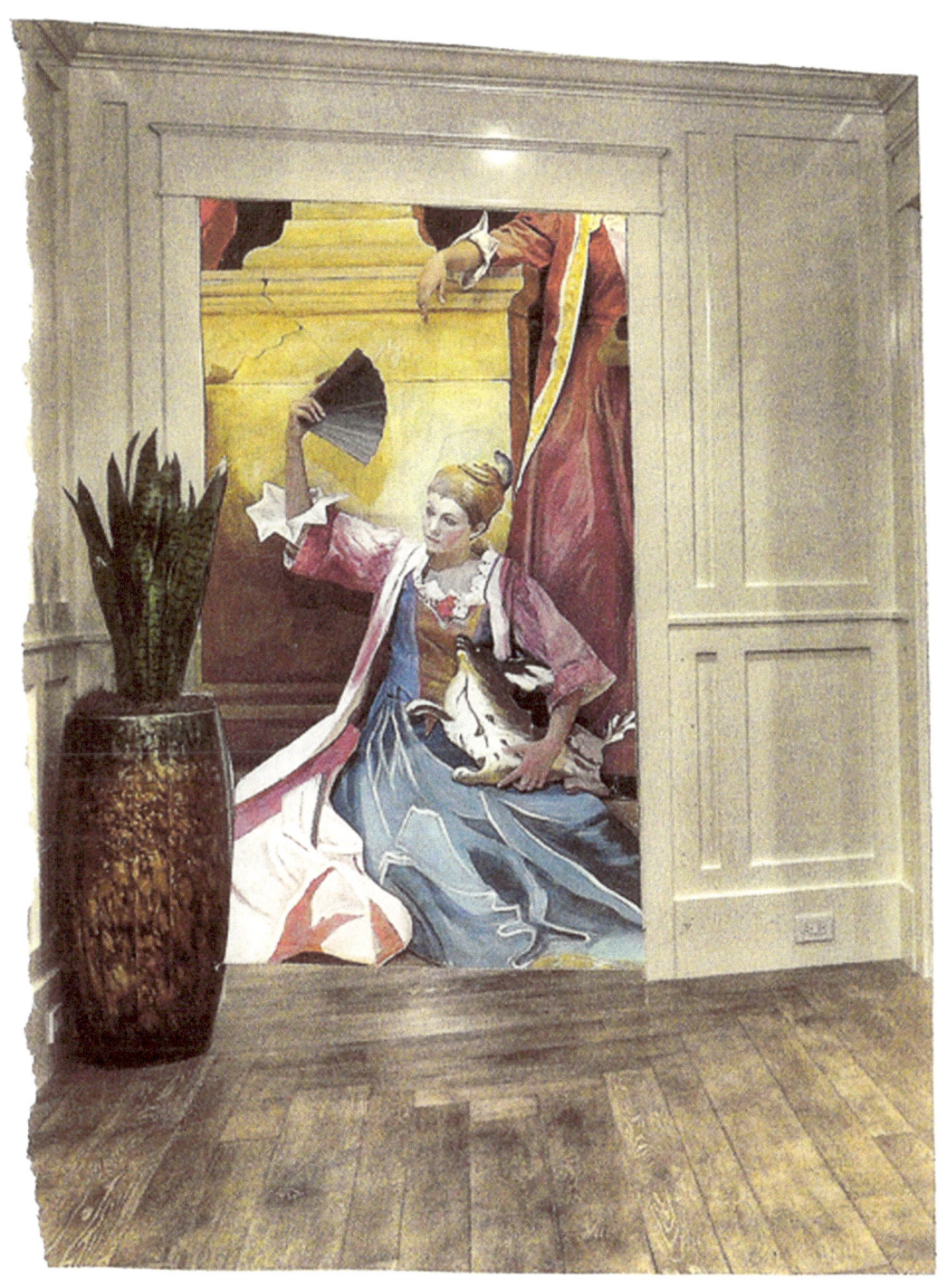

View, 8x5.5"

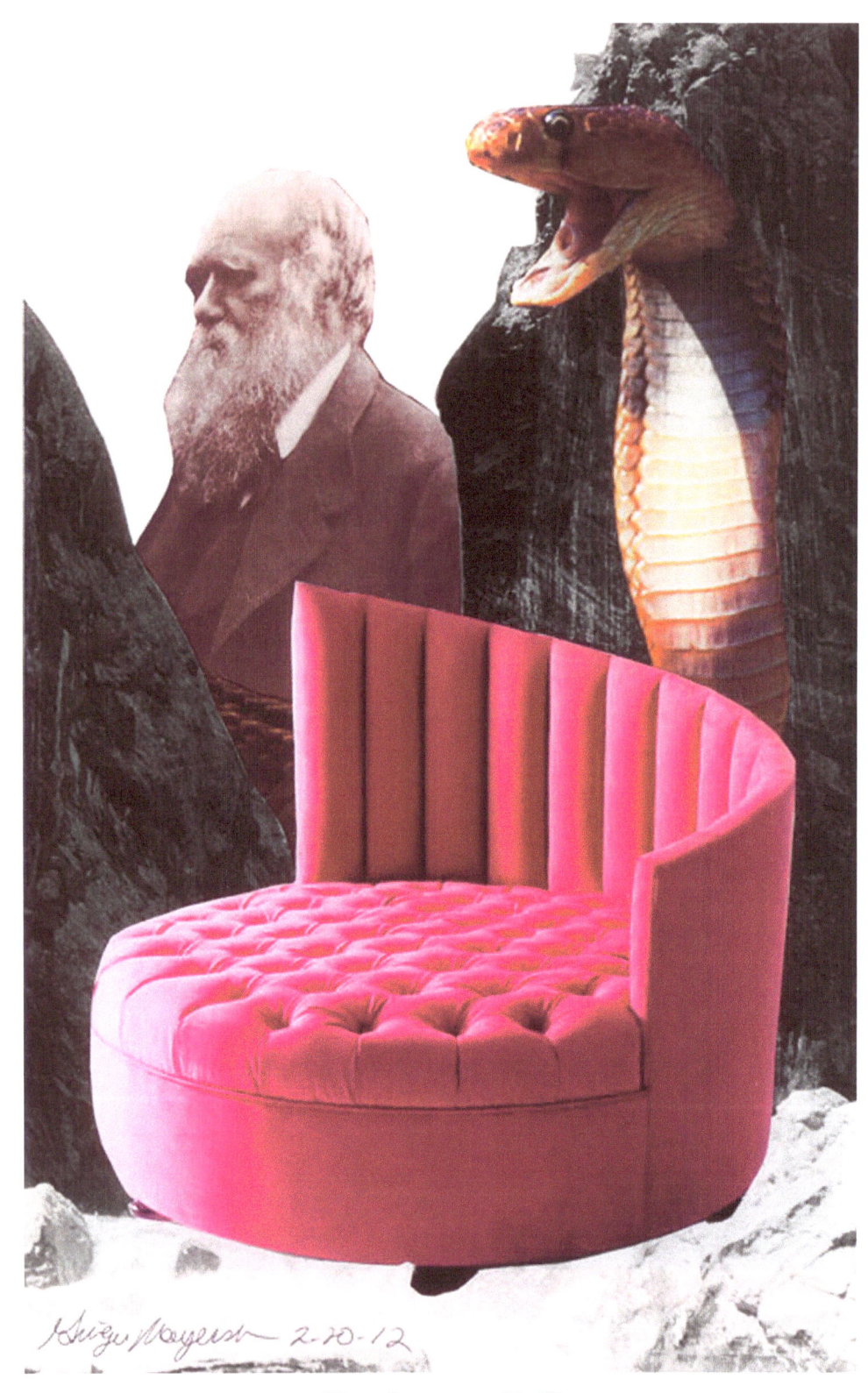

Viper Loveseat, 10x7"

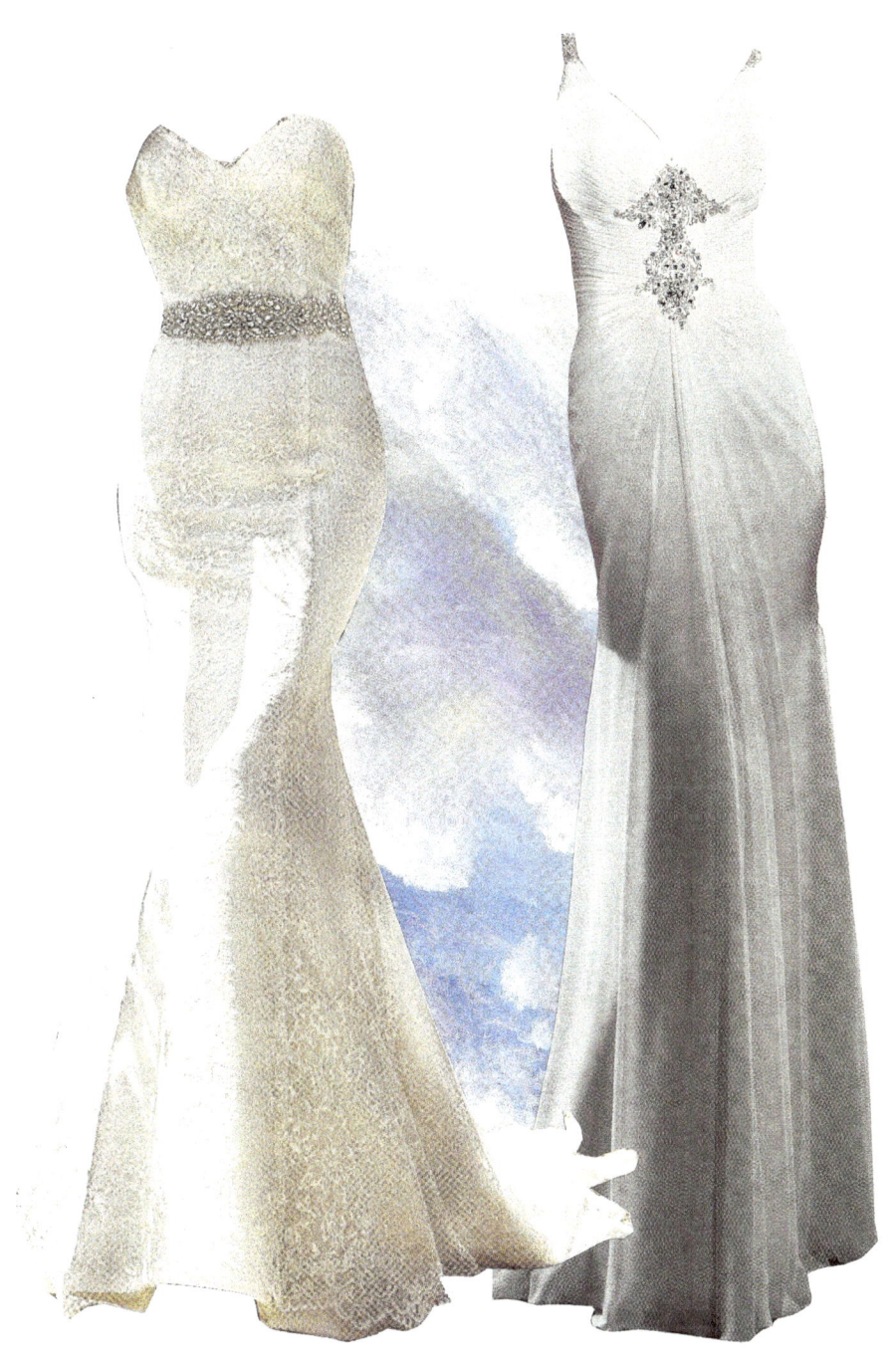

Wedding Dresses in the Sky, 10x7"

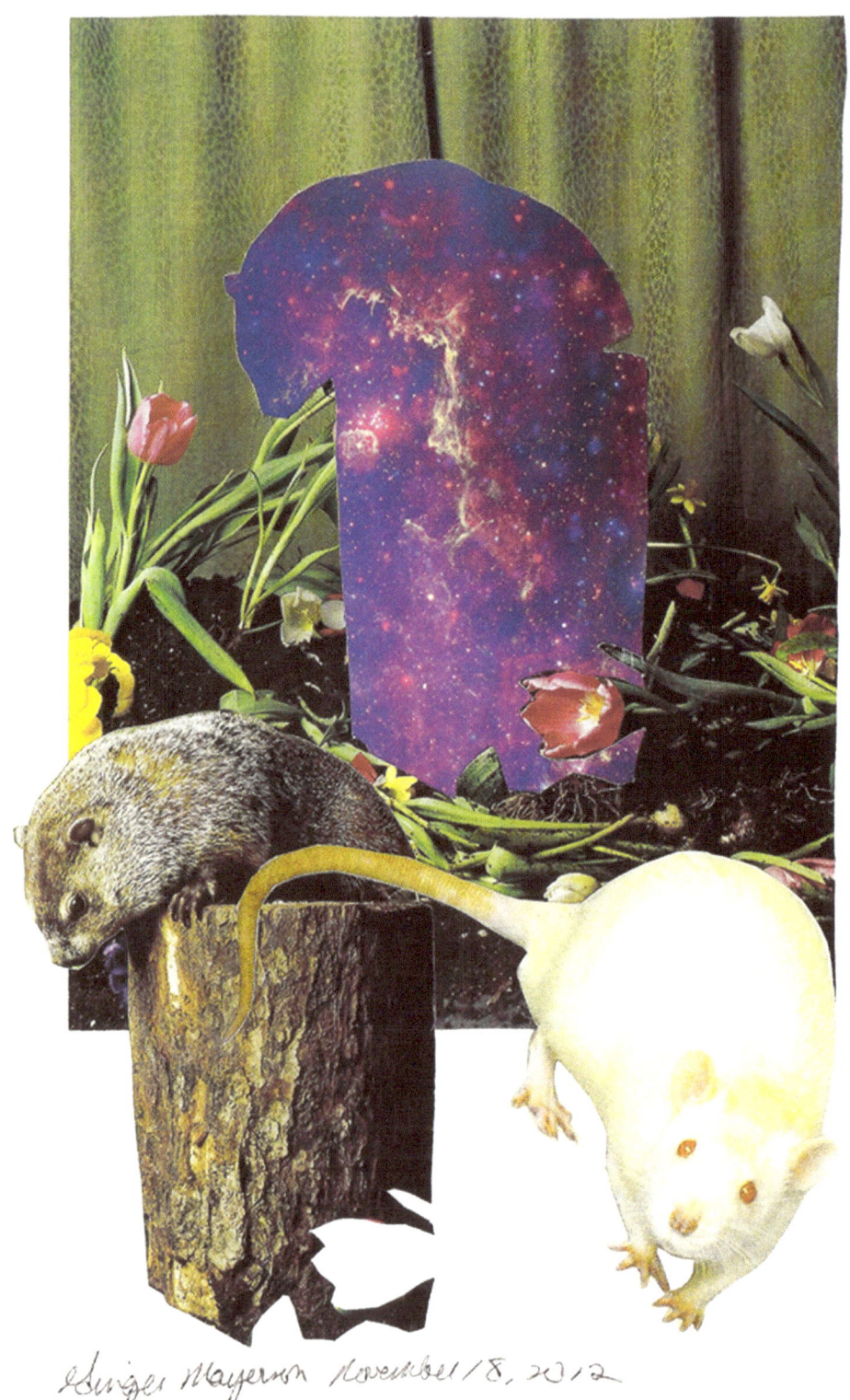

Wilderness Rat, 8x5.5"

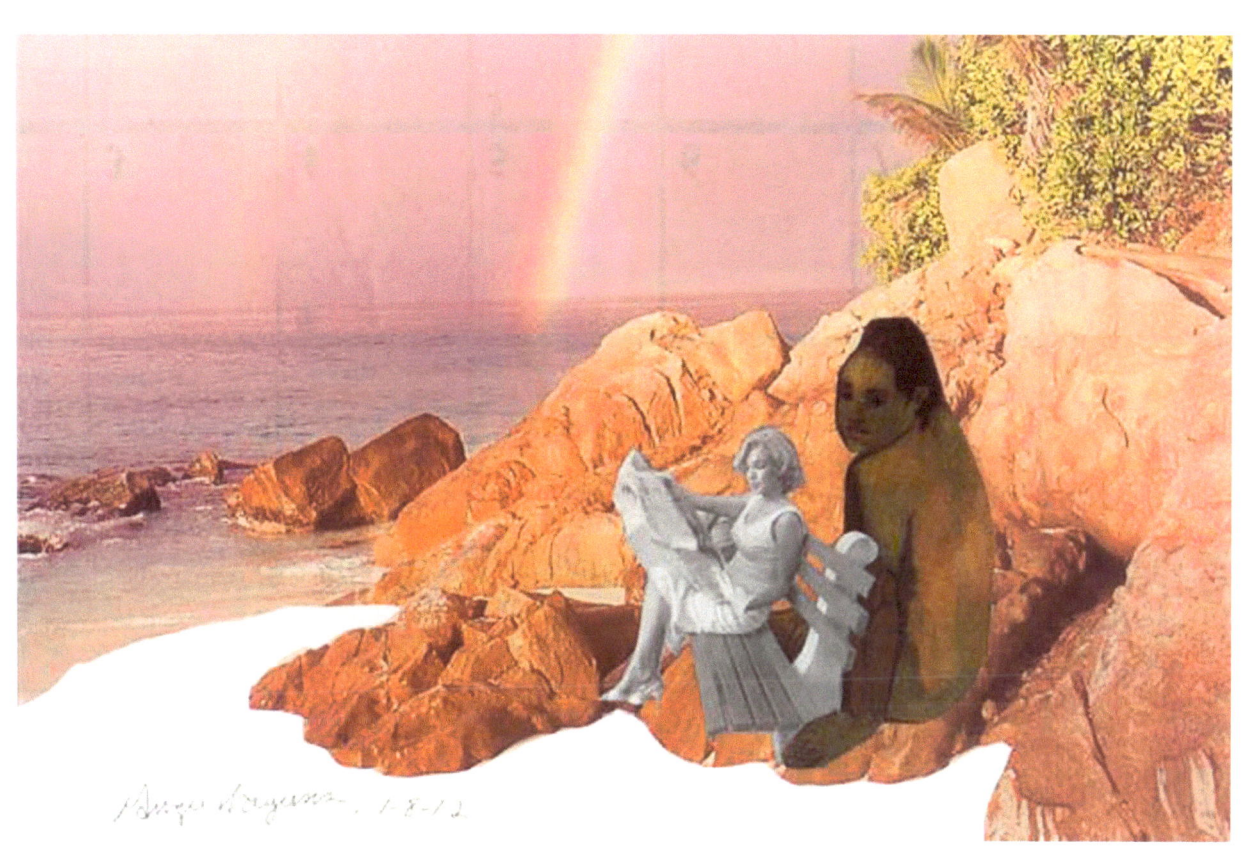

What's the Date on that Newspaper? 10x7"

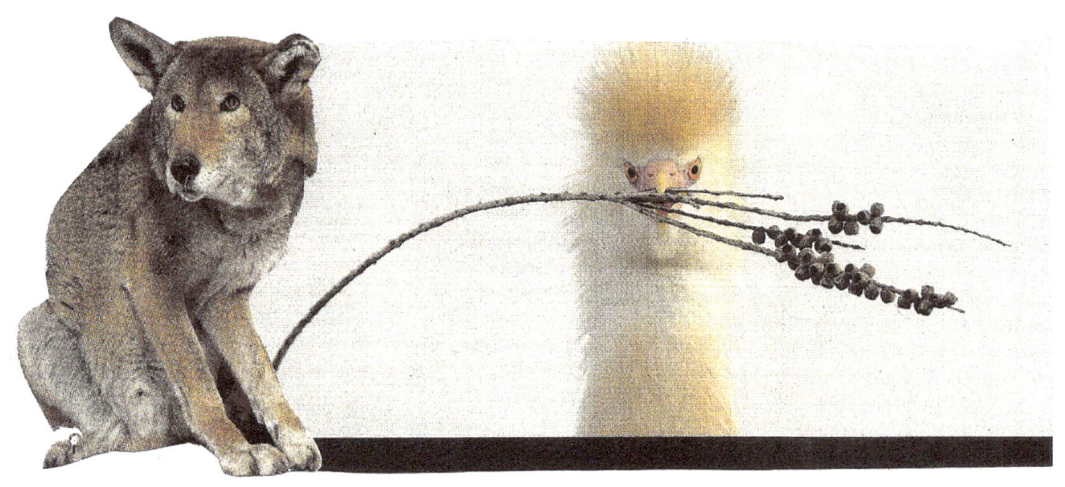

Wolf Bird, 4x6"

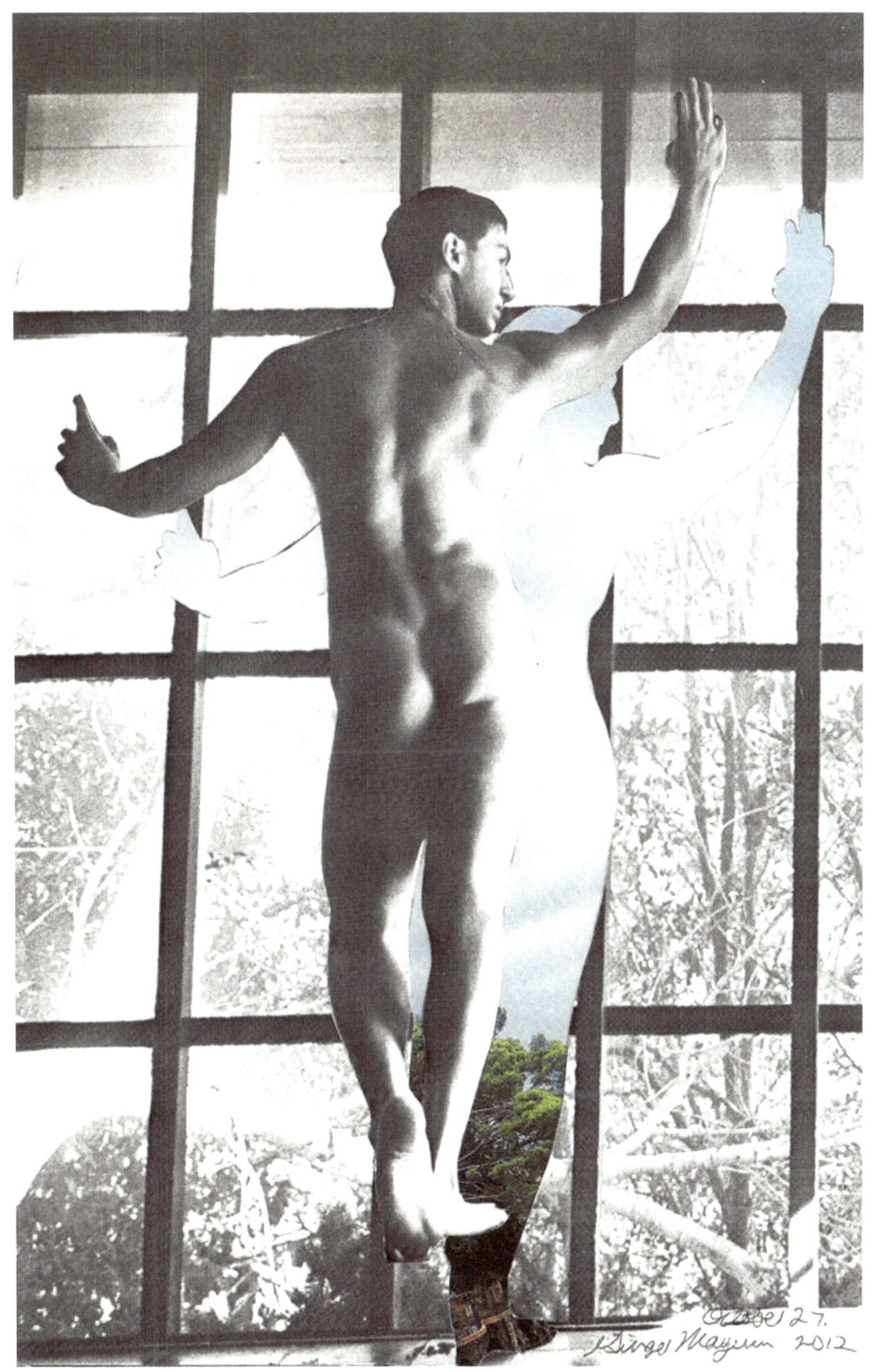

Window, 10x7"

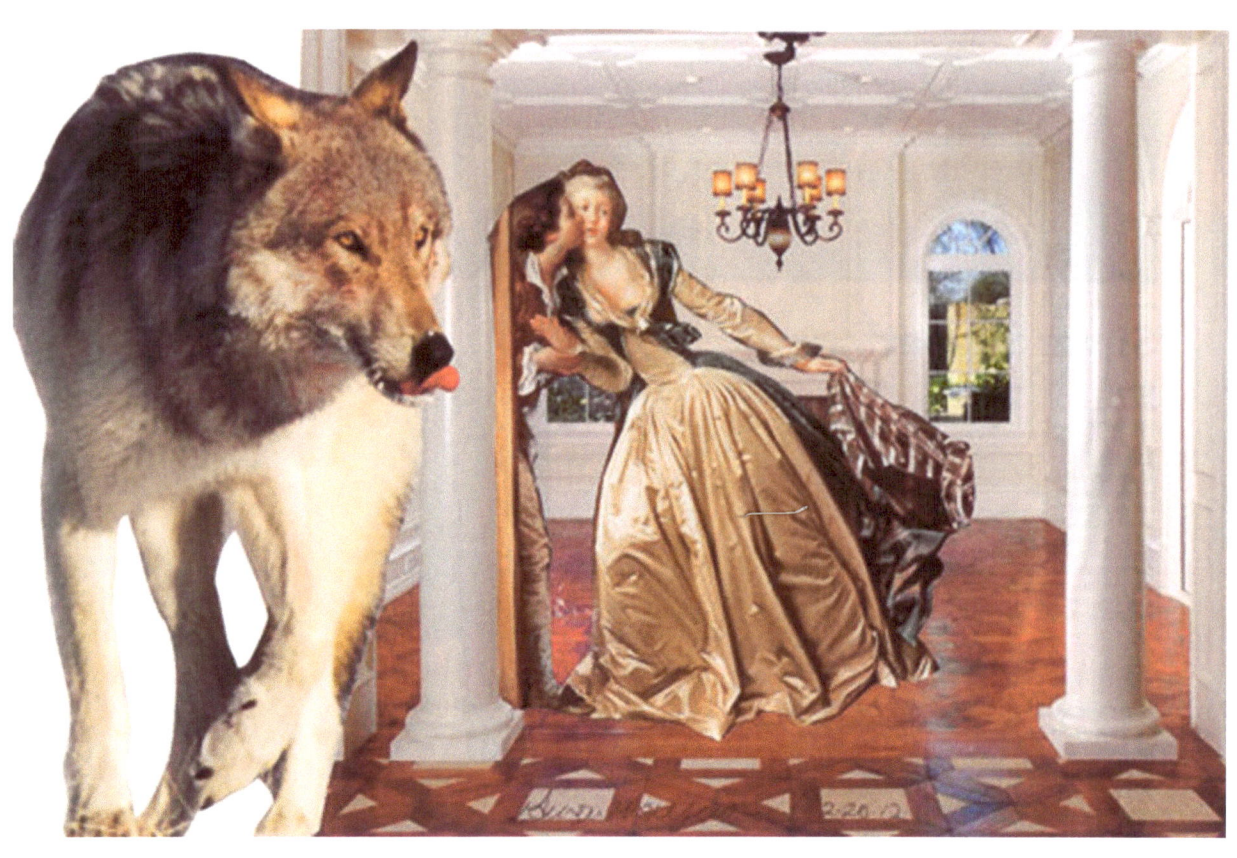

Wolf View, 7x10"

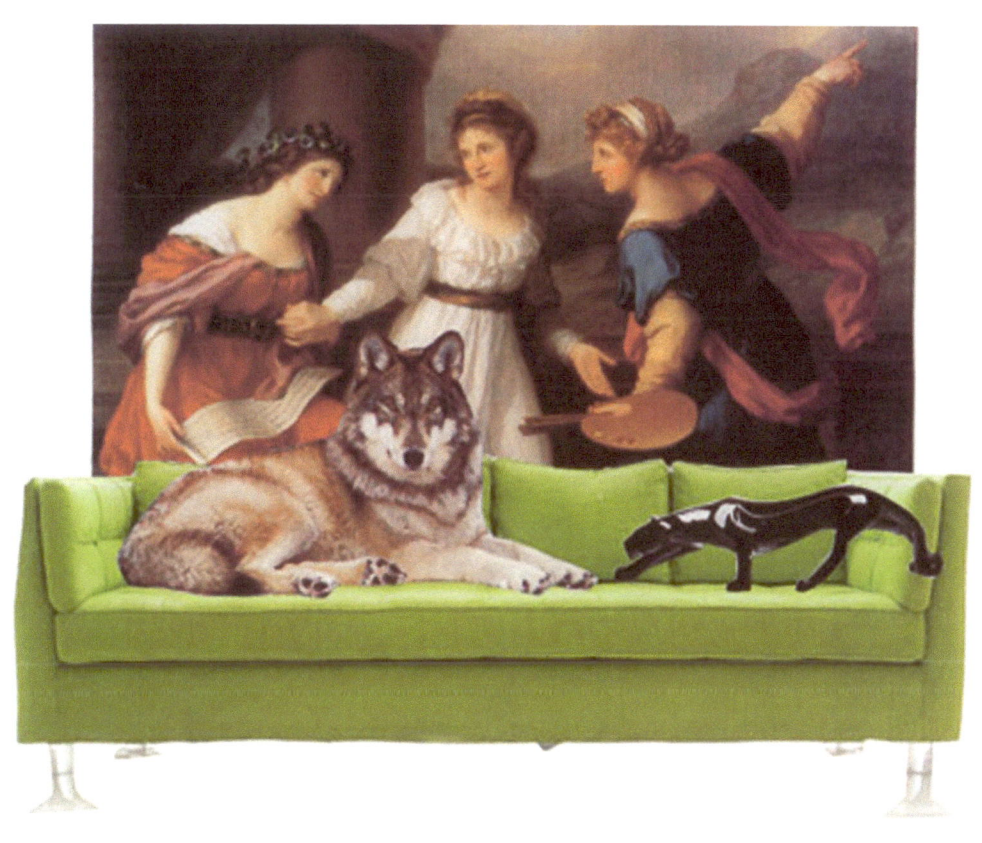

Wolf Couch, 7x10"

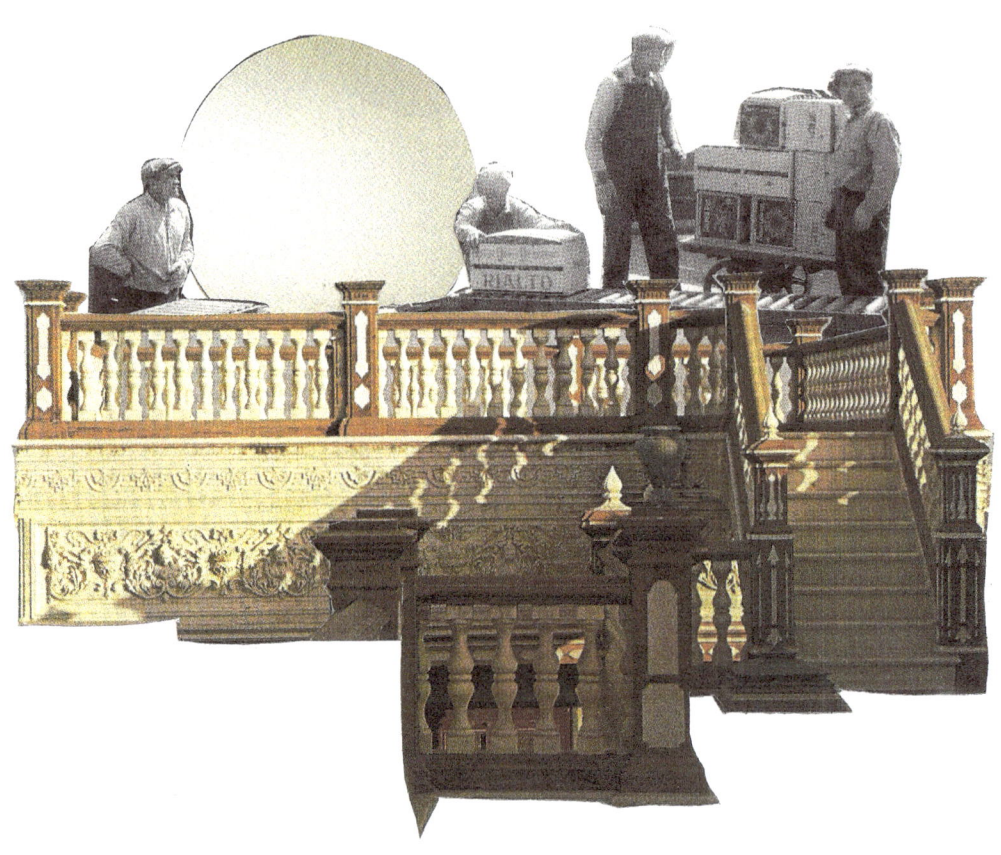

Worker Balcony, 8x5.5"

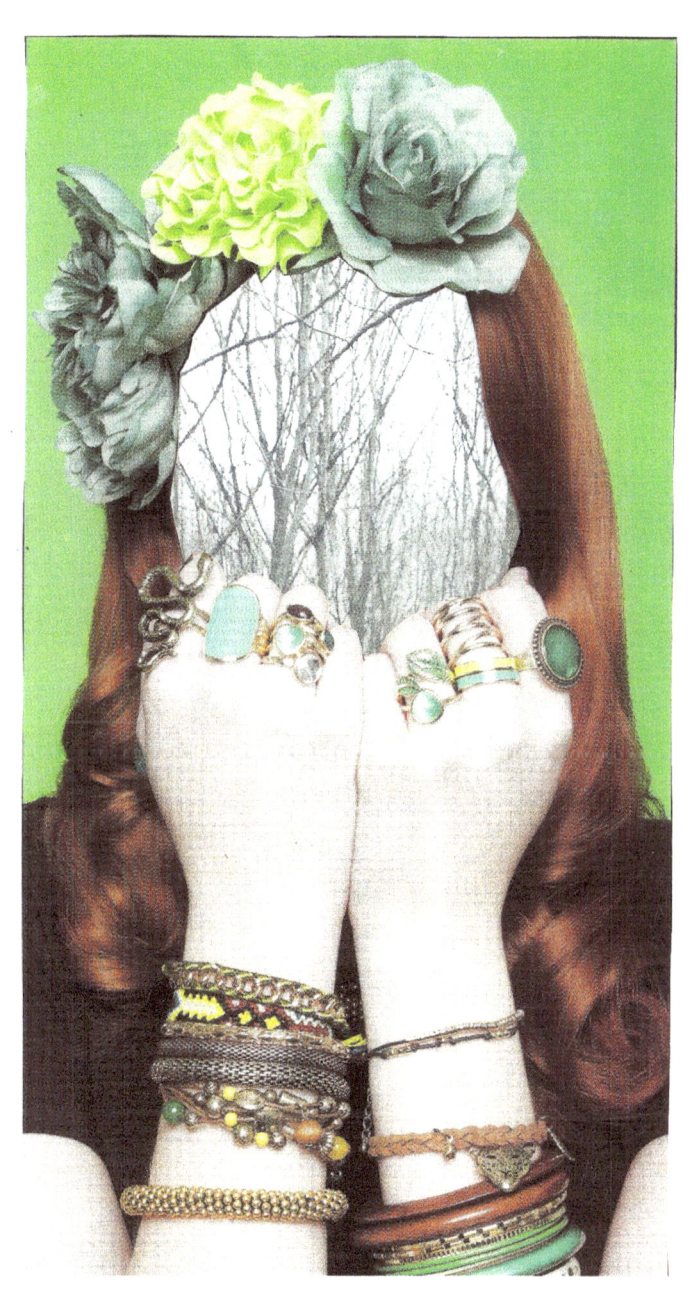

Woods, 10x7"

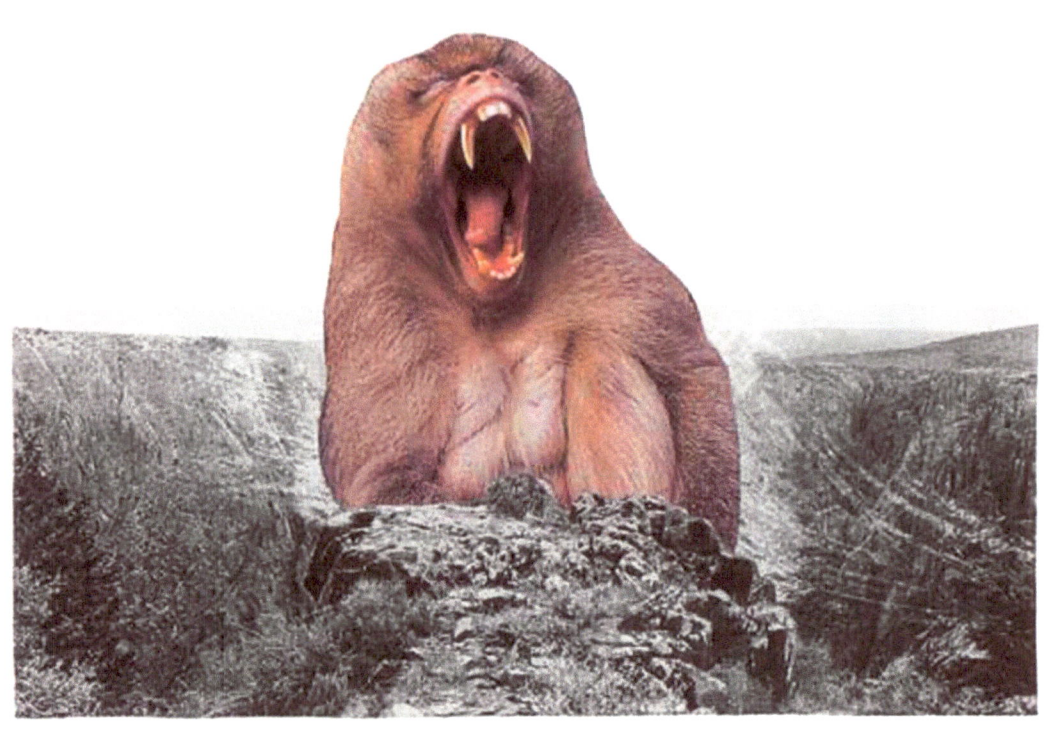

Yawn or Scream? 8x5.5"

www.ingramcontent.com/pod-product-compliance
Lightning Source LLC
Chambersburg PA
CBHW051154220526
45473CB00003B/774